毎日の英速読
頭の中に「英文読解の回路」をつくる

James M. Vardaman・神崎正哉

朝日新聞出版

朗読音声について

本書の朗読音声))) は、
下記 URL から自由にダウンロードできます。

検索方法
朝日新聞出版 🔍
↓
朝日新聞出版ホームページのトップページ右上の
検索欄に「毎日の英速読」と入力してください
↓
「毎日の英速読」のページから、
パソコンで音声データをダウンロードしてください

URL：
http://publications.asahi.com/ecs/
detail/?item_id=15998

＊音声ダウンロードは、パソコン回線で行ってください。
スマートフォンや MP3 プレーヤーでご使用の場合は、
パソコンにダウンロードしたデータを転送してください。

編集協力	Karl Rosvold
	及川亜也子
録音協力	英語教育協議会
	東 健一
ナレーション	Howard Colefield（米）
イラスト	齋藤太郎

毎日の英速読

頭の中に「英文読解の回路」をつくる

もくじ

本書の効用	005
トレーニング・メニュー	019
進捗の軌跡	024
速読トレーニング	029

UNIT 01	Learning from the Bears	031
UNIT 02	Juan the Bear	039
UNIT 03	GDP Man	047
UNIT 04	The Camera Thief	055
UNIT 05	The New Breadwinner	063
UNIT 06	Keeping an Eye on You	070
UNIT 07	Revolution in Color	079
UNIT 08	Under the Sea	087
UNIT 09	The Right Sound	095
UNIT 10	Musical Medicine	103
UNIT 11	Coming Up with Ideas	111
UNIT 12	Playing at Work?	119
UNIT 13	Creating a Voice	127
UNIT 14	To Like or Not to Like	135
UNIT 15	3D Printing	143
UNIT 16	Give Them a Hand	151
UNIT 17	Education for What?	159
UNIT 18	Have You Done Your Homework?	167
UNIT 19	The Ideal Translator	175
UNIT 20	Speaking Two Languages	183
+	カポーティに触れる	191

本書の効用

村上春樹も
ぽりぽり読んだ

　英語の速読は、どうすれば身につくのか。

　それに対する答えを、村上春樹さんの発言の中に見つけました。

　村上さんは、毎年のようにノーベル文学賞候補に名前が挙がる世界的な小説家ですが、翻訳者としても旺盛な活躍をされています。

　J.D. サリンジャー『キャッチャー・イン・ザ・ライ』、

　トルーマン・カポーティ『ティファニーで朝食を』、

　レイモンド・チャンドラー『ロング・グッドバイ』、

　レイモンド・カーヴァー『頼むから静かにしてくれ』、

　マイケル・ギルモア『心臓を貫かれて』、

　など、小説だけでなくノン・フィクションも含めた数多くの翻訳を手掛けられています。また、村上さんの小説の文体がアメリカ文学の影響も受けていることは、自他ともに認めるところです。村上さんご自身は「語学が苦手だ」とおっしゃっていますが、アメリカの有名大学で教鞭をとっていらっしゃったくらいですから、相当達者なはずです。

　その証拠に、エルサレム賞授賞式において、現地に赴いて行ったスピーチ "Always on the side of the egg"（「いつも卵の側に」）ですばらしい英語を使われていました。かてて加えて、"Between a high, solid wall and an egg that breaks against it, I will stand on the side of the egg"（「高くて堅い壁とそれにぶつかって割れる卵があるとしたら、僕はいつも卵の側でありたい」、つま

り、文学として常に弱い側に立っていたい）と宣言したその内容によって、世界中の人々の胸を打ったものです。村上さんの小説と同じく、やさしくわかりやすい表現でありながら核心をつく彼の言葉の力に感嘆したことを覚えています。

さて、以下は、『翻訳夜話』（文藝春秋）という書籍で翻訳家の柴田元幸さんと対話した際のものです。

> 「英語の勉強って専門的にしたことは一度もないんです。僕は小説を読むのが好きだから、英語の小説はもう高校時代からどんどん読んでたんだけど、それは非常に非常に乱暴な読み方で、デリカシーとか正確さとかそんなものはかけらもない読み方でした。**頭からぼりぼり貪り食うみたいな読み方**です。でもとにかく手当たり次第に頭から尻尾まで読みまくった。高校生のときは英語の成績だってそんなに良くなかったです、正直な話。勉強といっても**自分の好きなことしかやらなかった**から。」（＊太字は筆者による）

村上さんは、好きな英文小説を「頭からぼりぼり貪り食うみたいに」読んだといいます。それなのに、「好きなことしかやらなかったから学校の成績は良くなかった」と。

ここには、速読力をつけるためのキーワードが3つ入っています。それは、

「頭からぼりぼり」
「貪り食うみたいに」
「好きなことしかやらない」

です。

「頭からぼりぼり」というのは、**英文を英語の語順のママで読み進めている**、ということ。
　「貪り食うみたいに」とは、**とにかく何でもたくさん読む**、ということ。
　「好きなことしかやらない」ということは、角度を変えると、**好きなことは長続きする**、ということです。
　これらはすべて、速読力をつけるトレーニングに欠かせないものです。身も蓋もありませんが、シンプルに言ってしまえば、**たくさん読めば読んだ分だけ読むスピードは速くなる**、のです。私も日本語が読めるようになったのは、好きな小説やエッセイを数多く読んできたからでしょう。今も、朝日新聞を毎日読んでおりますし、『明暗』『雁』『吉原御免状』など小説も読みます。英語では *National Geographic*, *Smithsonian*, *The Atlantic*, *Economist*, *International New York Times* などを読んでいます。村上さんも、好きな小説をたくさん読んで読めるようになったのでしょう。
　そこには種も仕掛けもないのです。

　速読というと、「フォト・リーディング」のような何か特別な方法があるのではないか、と思っている方もいるでしょう。映画「レインマン」のモデルとなったという、サヴァン症候群のキム・ピーク氏は、電話帳のページを数十秒見ただけでそのページすべての番号を暗記してしまいます。彼らは一瞬で、まるで瞼でシャッターを切るように、脳の中に見たままの正確な文字情報をダウンロードコピーしてしまえるのです。世の中で喧伝されている「速読術」は、そのような能力をイメージしているのかもしません。
　けれど、われわれが身につけるべき速読はそんな特殊な能力ではありません。繰り返しますが、読む速さは読んだ量に比例して速くなっていくものです。
　繰り返しこそが力となり、速読力を涵養します。

しかし、そこにまったくコツがないわけではありません。

科学的、心理学的にも理に適った方法があります。

魔法のような方法はありませんが、私が母語ではない日本語を速く読めるようになった経験、30年以上にわたって日本の大学生に英語を教えてきた経験を踏まえ、「速読」できるようになるための効率的なトレーニング方法をご紹介いたします。

「トレーニング・メニュー」については、TOEIC講師として圧倒的な実績を積まれ、速読トレーニング指導に大変力を入れておられる神崎正哉先生と共に、お互い学生に最も効果が出た共通の方法をご紹介しています。

日本人の「英語必要係数」

社会人のためのカルチャースクールで英語の講座を開くと、熱心な学習者が多くいらっしゃいます。「会社で英語が必要になった」というビジネスパーソンが増えているのです。仕事で英語が必要な状況は様々だと思いますが、そこで求められるのはどんな力でしょう。

私は、本当に英語がないと仕事にならない、という正味の「英語必要係数」は、これまで、日本人ビジネスパーソン全体の5％にも満たなかったのではないかと思っています。

明治の開国以来、日本は日本語によって守られてきました。当時から人口3千万人を超え、現在1億2千万人超を誇る日本語経済圏の中にいれば、英語ができなくてもその中で十分に経済的な豊かさを享受できたのでしょう。

しかしながら、周知のように、ビジネスパーソンの英語必要係数

は否応なく上がっています。IT機器とネットワークの指数関数的な発達に比例して、ビジネス界は加速度的にグローバル化しています。ギリシャがくしゃみをすればアメリカが咳をし、日本企業が風邪を引く事態が当然のごとく散見される状況です。

そのような中で、ビジネスパーソンは、世界の新しい情報により速く、正確に触れ、取捨選択し、自分なりの情報を編んでいくことが求められます。

実際の仕事の現場では、

- 取引先からのメールの趣旨は何か
- そのメールは重要なものなのか、そうではないのか
- 業界通信に注目すべき情報はないか
- 海外ニュースにアイデアの種はないか
- ある事項の海外での評判はどうか

というように、大量の英文メールや資料を読み、瞬時に判断して優先順位をつけなくてはならないのが日常です。

ビジネスの最前線に立って、家族や日本という国を養っていこうというとき、日本語によって加工された２次情報ではなく、斬れば血の出るような１次情報の英語を扱っていかざるを得ません。「以心伝心」は通用しません。待ったなしの仕事の最前線では、スピードが生命線です。仕事の現場では、日本語（母語）・英語（外国語）に関係なく、「有益な情報をピックアップする能力」が求められます（われわれ研究者の世界も同様です。理系はもちろん、文系の論文も英語が主流です）。

会議や電話での英会話、英文メールのやりとりなど、アウトプットを含む英語コミュニケーション能力はその先にあります。まずは、情報や相手の言い分を理解することが先決です。つまり、「英文速読力」は仕事で必要とされる英語力の基本なのです。そして、後で詳

述しますが、「速く、正確に英文を読むインプット力」を養うことが、ひいてはアウトプットの能力も高めることとなります。

　私は日本とビジネス界の現実をそのように捉えておりますが、「そんなことはとてもできませんよ！」と思っていらっしゃる方も多いかもしれません。あるいは、仕事でなく、国際交流や教養として英語を身につけようとしておられる意識の高い方にとっても、なかなか高いハードルかもしれません。
　でも大丈夫です。継続できさえすれば、誰にでもできるようになります。
　momentum という英単語がキーワードです。「推進力」を意味する言葉で、gain momentum（はずみがつく、勢いがつく）というように使います。
　本書で、自分の納得のいく「英文速読」ができるようになるための勢いをつけてください。「英文読解の回路」を脳の中につくって、「持続可能なトレーニング」の習慣をつけるのです。
　「英文読解の回路」の基礎ができてしまえば、英語を英語の語順のまま理解することができるようになります。できるようになった学生に聞いても、私の日本語の読解習得の過程を思い返してみても、それは心躍る楽しい経験です。外国語で知識を得ることの快感を、ぜひとも味わってください。
　そのために、「正しい方法で英文を読むクセ」を自分の脳に刻み込むトレーニングをしましょう。それが、本書です。

　皆さんは母語である日本語を読みつけていますから、英語を「頭からぼりぼり読む」といってもはじめは大変だと思います。中学・高校・大学と一応英語の勉強をしてそのままという方が多いかもしれません。それは、車に例えればエンストして止まっているような状況です。エンストの車にエンジンをかけるためには、後ろから押

すといいでしょう。一度エンジンがかかってしまえば後はスムーズに進んでいきます。本書のトレーニングは、強力な推進力となります。

　行動は習慣を生み、習慣は新たな思考を生み、自分を変えていきます。ぜひ、英語の読める自分に変わってください。

　それは、必ずできます。

どのくらいの速さで読めればいいか？

　昨今、日本企業が英語コミュニケーション能力を計るために取り入れている試験にTOEIC（Test of English for International Communication）があります。国内受験者は、年間のべ230万人を超え、2012年の日本の平均スコアは990点満点で512点、韓国は628点、中国は747点となっています。日本の平均スコアはなぜ低いのでしょう。

　私が働いている大学のアジア人留学生は、母語と日本語に加え、当然のように英語も習得しています。できない者は、それこそ目の色を変えて励んでいます。リクルートスーツに身を包んで就職活動をしているのは日本の学生だけではありません。彼らも、日本でチャンスをつかもうとしています。日本の学生はすでに、彼らに伍して仕事を獲得していかなければなりません。その傾向は今後ますます強まるでしょう。

　閑話休題。TOEICの日本人受験者の圧倒的多数が、テスト時間内に最後まで問題を終えることができないといいます。問題数が多すぎて、途中で時間切れになってしまうそうです。これは、言うまでもなく、英語を読むスピードが不足しているからです。

もちろん、TOEICはあくまで一つのテストですから、TOEICのスコアを上げればいいというものではありませんが、それにしても平均点が半分そこそこというのはいただけません。

　では、どのくらいの速度で読めれば、問題を最後まで解き終えることができるのか。TOEICの専門家である共著の神崎先生にお聞きしたところ、およそ1分間に150語（150〜180 words/minute）読むことができれば、時間内にTOEICの問題をすべて読んで回答することができるそうです。

　この速さは、ネイティブスピーカーが普通に話す速さとほぼ同じです。衛星テレビで見ることができるCNNなどのニュースキャスターは、およそ180〜200 words/minuteの速さですので、それよりはゆっくりですが、日本人が生の英語を聞くとかなり速く感じるかもしれません。

　しかし、日本の英語教材は、やや丁寧に読んでいるものが多く、120 words/minute前後のものが一般的です。本書のテキストの朗読音声は少し丁寧に読んでいますが、それでも英語ネイティブのナチュラルスピードを心がけていますので140〜160 words/minuteくらいの速さです。

　ですから、はじめは本書のナレーターが読む速さと同じ速さで、読んで意味が理解できるようになることを目標にするのがいいでしょう。後戻りしないで音声と同じ速さで読むことができたら、140〜160 words/minuteの速読力があるということです。

　その速さで読めるようになれば、「英文読解の回路」の基礎部分はできているといってもいいでしょう。

「英文読解の回路」をつくろう

　ご自身も30歳までは英語ができなかったという米Google副社長を務めていらっしゃった村上憲郎さんは、はじめは100 words/minuteだった速さが、1日30分から1時間、毎日英文を読み続けることによって、200、300 words/minuteと上がっていったといいます。以下は、『村上式　シンプル英語勉強法』（ダイヤモンド社）からの引用です。

　　最初100ワード/分ぐらいからスタートしても、これが読むうちに200ワード/分になり、300ワード/分になってくる。この頃には徐々に頭の中の音読が黙読になってきます。
　　もちろん、最初は読むスピードも右肩上がりに速くはなりません。しかし1日30分から1時間。**毎日読み続ければ、あるとき突然「あれ、速くなってきた」という時期がきます**。個人差はありますが1カ月から2カ月くらいごとに変化が訪れます。（＊太字は筆者による）

　200 words/minute、300 words/minuteとぽんぽんと言われてもできる実感が湧かないかもしれませんが、そんなことはありません。**あるとき突然、「あれ、速くなってきた」という時期**がポイントです。村上憲郎さんもご自身で「英文は後戻りして読んではいけない」とおっしゃっていますが、それは、それまで無理矢理頭から読んでいた英文が、自然に頭から読めるようになった瞬間だったのでしょう。ここで「英文読解の回路」が脳の中に出来上がったのです。

リスニングで
「英文読解の回路」をつくる

　大変前置きが長くなりました。いよいよ「英文読解の回路」をつくるコツをご紹介します。
　ポイントは、

> ・リスニングをすること。
> ・目だけでなく耳と口を活用すること。

　前述のように、本書の朗読スピードは 140〜160 words/minute です。音声を聞きながら、その速さで英文を目で追ってください。
　朗読音声は後戻りしません。耳で音声を聞きながらその部分の英文を読むようにすると、否応なく英文を頭から読まざるを得なくなります。
　リスニングは、「発音・アクセント・英文の音の強弱・音のつながりと変化」といった「正しい英語の音とリズム」を頭の中にしみ込ませることができる英語習得の肝です。英文を聞きながら速読を意識することによって、耳で音のトレーニングをすると同時に、英文リーディングの鉄則である「英文を頭から読む」トレーニングを行うことができるのです。
　まさに、一石二鳥です。
　目と耳と正しい音声。意識的な「リスニング＆速読」によって「英文読解の回路」を脳の中につくります。

架け橋となる
スラッシュ・リーディング

　しかしながら、まだ英語に取り組みはじめたばかりの方や、初級・中級者の方は、なかなか朗読スピードについていくことが難しいと思います。これまで英語のトレーニングをしてこなかったのですから当然のことです。

　その場合は、「スラッシュ・リーディング」のテキストと音声を活用してください。

　英文は、カンマやピリオドの箇所以外にも、小さい意味のかたまりやフレーズで細かく区切ることができます。本書は、そこの区切りにスラッシュを入れ、さらにスラッシュ毎の意味を「ルビ訳」として英語の上に記しました。

マヤはとてもいい案を思いついた　　その本のシリーズタイトルの
Maya has a very good idea ／ for the book series title. ∥

　このくらいの単文ならすぐに頭から理解できるかもしれませんが、長い英文や、単文ではなくまとまった文章になると、どこかで理解につまずいて、後戻りしてしまいたくなる場合があります。そのときに助けとなるのが、スラッシュとその「ルビ訳」です。

　いきなり「素のテキスト」でリスニングをしながら速読するのが難しい場合は、こちらを使ってください。朗読音声も、通常のものに加え、スラッシュ毎にブレスを入れたものを用意しました。

　ただ、その場合も「ルビ訳」はなるべく見ないようにしてください。あくまで、意味がわからなくて「あれっ？」と思ったときだけ、

ヒント感覚で、目の端にある「ルビ訳」を見るようにしてください。

英語の読解テストで、途中で意味がわからなくなって、同じ英文を何度も繰り返し読んだことがあると思います。そのとき、頭の中で日本語に翻訳して、「戻り読み」を繰り返していたのではありませんか？

それは「日本語的な英文読解」です。そのクセを直すには、ぜったいに後戻りしない「音声」を活用するのがいちばんなのです。

強制的に頭から読むトレーニングです。

「戻り読み」はぜったいに禁止ですから。

はじめはできない方も、スラッシュ・リーディングから繰り返せば、必ず頭から読めるようになります。

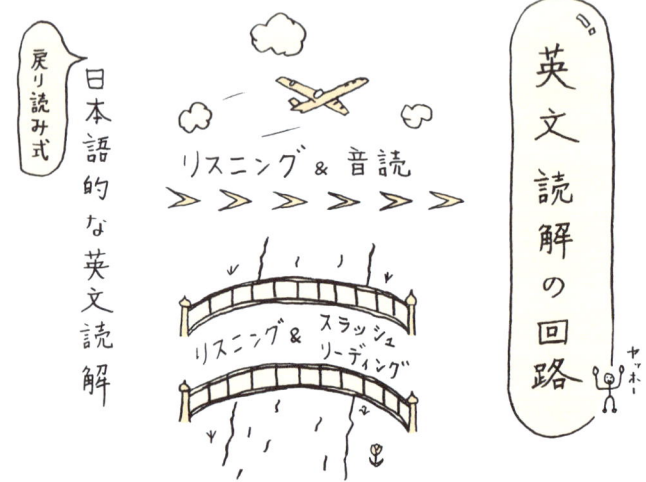

速読から
アウトプットへ

　「英文読解の回路」をつくるトレーニングには、その先があります。「リスニング&速読」では目と耳を使いました。今度は、口も使って、より堅固な「英文読解の回路」をつくりましょう。

　前著、『毎日の英文法』『毎日の英単語』で、「口を動かして実際に話す練習をしなければ、ぜったいに英会話などできるようにならない」と申しました。そして、音読の効用も記しました（本書の音声ダウンロードページに、『毎日の英文法』の「本書の効用」を無料でアップしています）。

　具体的な方法としては、朗読音声を追いかけるように声に出す「シャドーイング」と「音読」を行ってください。目で理解し、耳で音を捉え、口に出して英語を脳に刻み込むのです。

　『毎日の英文法』や『毎日の英単語』でつくり上げた「英文の核となるパターン・表現」を、本書のまとまった英文テキストでならす
・・
ように統合し、自分の英語力の核となる豊かな厚みにしてください。

　センテンスや、フレーズ単位だった「使える英語」の素材を、自分の血肉とするのです。

　フレーズではなくセンテンスを、単文ではなく複文を、口に出すことにより、よりまとまった英語表現をアウトプットする練習となります。

　何事も「習うより慣れよ」と申します。私は日本語のお手本をつくることはできませんが、トレーニングに堪え得る英語のテキストはつくれます。ぜひ、本書の英文をご自分の英語表現の踏み台として活用できるよう、口に出すトレーニングを行ってください。

速読トレーニング用
テキスト

　本書のテキストは、速読トレーニング用に作成しました。特徴は、単語のレベルを 2000 語レベルにしてあることです。

　使われている単語は、固有名詞などを除いて『毎日の英単語』がカバーしているリストの範囲内の単語です。そのリストは、ネイティブの日常会話に使われる単語の頻度を優先し、West's General Service List や Bank of English などのコーパスを分析して作成しました。また、Academic Word List、University Word List からは高校・大学・新聞などで特によく使う単語も加えてあります（詳細は『毎日の英単語』をご参照ください）。

　非英語ネイティブに対する英語教授法の研究によると、未知の英単語が全体の 5％以上あると、内容をスムーズに理解することができなくなるといいます。ですから、本書では、皆さんが身につけているべき上記リストの範囲内の単語を 95〜98％使ってテキストを作成しています。範囲外の単語は、それぞれの Unit のキーワードとして外せない単語です。たとえば、Unit2 の Zebra（シマウマ）などです。

　また、各 Unit のやや難しい表現を約 20 ずつ、各 Unit 扉のページに記載してあります。

　文書の長さは、実用性と読みやすさを考慮して 300 語程度としました。最終的には、このくらいの分量を 120 秒以内で読むことができるようになることをイメージしています。

　では、いよいよ具体的なトレーニング・メニューです。

トレーニング・メニュー

Step 1 速読の準備運動

「速読」をする前の大切な準備運動です。

本書には、全部で20のUnitがあります。それぞれのUnitには英語のタイトルと日本語のサブタイトルがついています。イメージイラストと合わせて、本文に何が書かれているか、おおよその予想をしてみましょう。

また、イラストの下にやや難しめの表現を約20掲載しました。一通り目を通して、わからない単語の意味を確認してください。

本書から離れて、生の英語の速読をする際も、予備知識や内容の予測は、大いに読解の助けとなります。

読む前に全体のイメージを想像することによって、英文の細部にこだわるのではなく、全体を読み、理解できるようになる訓練にもなります。

Step 2-1 目で読む

いよいよテキストです。

タイトルから、黙読で一気に読んでみましょう。

その際、**ご自分でテキストをすべて黙読する時間（秒数）を計ってください。**

すべて読み終えたら、26ページの「WPM(Words per minute)換算表」を見て、自分が1分間に何ワード読めたか確認し、テキストの右上に記入します。

わからなくても、歯を食いしばって目を先に動かしてください。全部を理解することが難しい方は、細部ではなく、全体的にどんな話なのかを捉える訓練をしましょう。

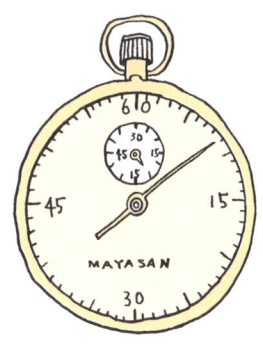

Step 2-2 True or False?

　本文がきちんと理解できたかどうかの簡単なテストです。
　答え合わせをして、3問以上間違えた方は、まだ全体の意味を捉えられていないかもしれません。その場合でも、いきなり和訳を見ずに、スラッシュ・リーディングのテキストでわからない箇所を特定し、その箇所の「ルビ訳」を見るようにしてください。

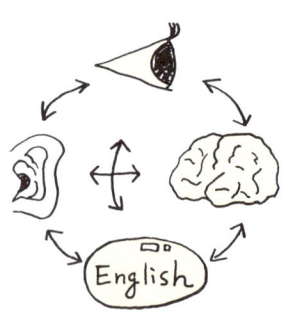

Step 3 目と耳で読む

　テキストの意味をすべて理解した上で、朗読音声を聴きながら、目でテキストを追ってください。
　まだわからない箇所がある場合は、スラッシュ・リーディングのテキストを見ながら朗読音声を聞いてください。
＊どうしてもわからない箇所がある場合は、「和訳」を確認したり、辞書を使ったりして、完全にすべてを理解し、その上で音声を一緒に聴いてください。

　朗読音声が速すぎてついていけない場合は、「スラッシュ・リーディング読み」をしている音声（Unit1の場合なら02）を聴きながら、スラッシュ・リーディングを読みましょう。

　耳で「発音・アクセント・英文の音の強弱・音のつながりと変化」といった「正しい英語の音とリズム」を聴き取りながら、そのリズムに合わせて目で速読します。
　そのUnitのすべてのテキストをスムーズに理解できるまで、「リスニング＆速読」を繰り返しましょう。

Step 4 口も鍛える（シャドーイング・音読）

さあ、最後の一ふんばりです。

このトレーニングをするかしないかが、より短期間で「英文読解の回路」をつくれるか否かの分かれ目です。

十分に「リスニング＆速読」を繰り返したら、今度は口も使いましょう。

朗読音声を追いかけるように、口真似をして、テキストを読んでください。

その際、テキストの意味をすべて理解しながら声に出しましょう。英文のリズムや抑揚まで真似することで、目、耳、口とあらゆる器官から脳に正しい英語を刻み込むことになります。

「シャドーイング」というトレーニングです。

何度か続けると、朗読音声よりも速く読むことができる方が出てくると思います。その場合は、朗読音声の音とリズムを崩さないように気をつけながら、音声を使わずに、ご自分で音読してみてください。

完全に理解した英文を、五感を使って脳に刻み込むことによって、「英文読解の回路」はもちろん、アウトプットの英語力も養成されます。

Step 5 進歩の記録

Step4まででトレーニング1周です。

もちろん、1周で終わるようなもったいないことはしないでください。2周、3周、4周、5周、6周と続けることで、堅固な「英文読解の回路」がつくられます。

そして、周回毎に、24ページの「進捗の軌跡」にWPMを記入してください。周回を重ねるたびに、進歩していく自分が見ることができるはずです。

その記録が、あきらめてしまいそうになった自分を励ましてくれる、何よりのトレーナーになっていきます。

本書を手にした皆さんなら、必ず、できます。

それでも
語るべき中身を

　最前線で世界と戦おうとするとき、英語はすでに十分条件ではなく、必要条件です。

　その上で、英語ができただけでは話になりません。前書の『毎日の英単語』でも記したように、英語の発音や文法の問題以前に、語るべき中身があるかどうか、が最も大切です。

　村上春樹さんは翻訳するにあたって、今でも「語学力」には自信がないといいます。しかし、なぜ翻訳に興味を持ったのかを聴かれ、こう答えておられました。

> 　結局、自分で文章を解体して、どうすればこういう素晴らしい文章を書けるのかということを、僕なりに解明したいという気持ちがあったんだと思います。英語の原文を日本語に置き換える作業を通して、何かそういう秘密のようなものを探り出したかったのかな。自分で実際に手を動かさないことにはわからないこと、身につかないことってありますよね。たとえば写経と同じようなもので。(『翻訳夜話』文藝春秋より)

　自分がどんな分野に興味を持ち、掘り下げていくことができるのか。アプローチもやり方も人それぞれ、まったく違います。けれど、興味や好奇心を持ったことに対して、「**自分で実際に手を動かす**」という態度で関わっていくことがその人の滋味となり、人物を形づくっていくのかもしれません。

　私が大変敬愛する作家のひとりにトルーマン・カポーティ氏がおります。村上春樹さんが、翻訳にいちばん最初に興味を持ったのは、高校時

代の参考書に載っていたカポーティの *The Headless Hawk*（無頭の鷹）の冒頭部分が「あまりにもその文章が見事なので、ひっくりかえるくらい感動した」からだそうです。そして、その当時「それを日本語に移し換えることによって、自分も主体的にその素晴らしさに参加しているというたしかな手応えがあった。カポーティもフィッツジェラルドにしても、非常に文章が精緻ですよね。美しくて、情感があって、確固としたスタイルがあって、そういうものを自分の手で日本語に移し換えることで、なんだか心が洗われるような喜びを感じることができた」と言うのです。

この言葉は、私にとって、カポーティの一ファンとしても、アメリカ文学研究者としても大変嬉しく感動を覚えるものでした。と同時に、村上春樹さんの豊かさを、肌で感じたのです。

本書のトレーニングをすれば、「英語読解の回路」をつくることができます。ぜひとも、それをご自分の道具の一つとして使い、社会の中や仕事や趣味の中で、自分なりの「実際に手を動かす」対象を見つけてください。

本書が、そのための momentum となることを心から願っております。

追記：本書の最後に、*The Headless Hawk* の冒頭の数行を掲載しました。

James M Vardaman

進捗の軌跡 ── WPM [words per minute]

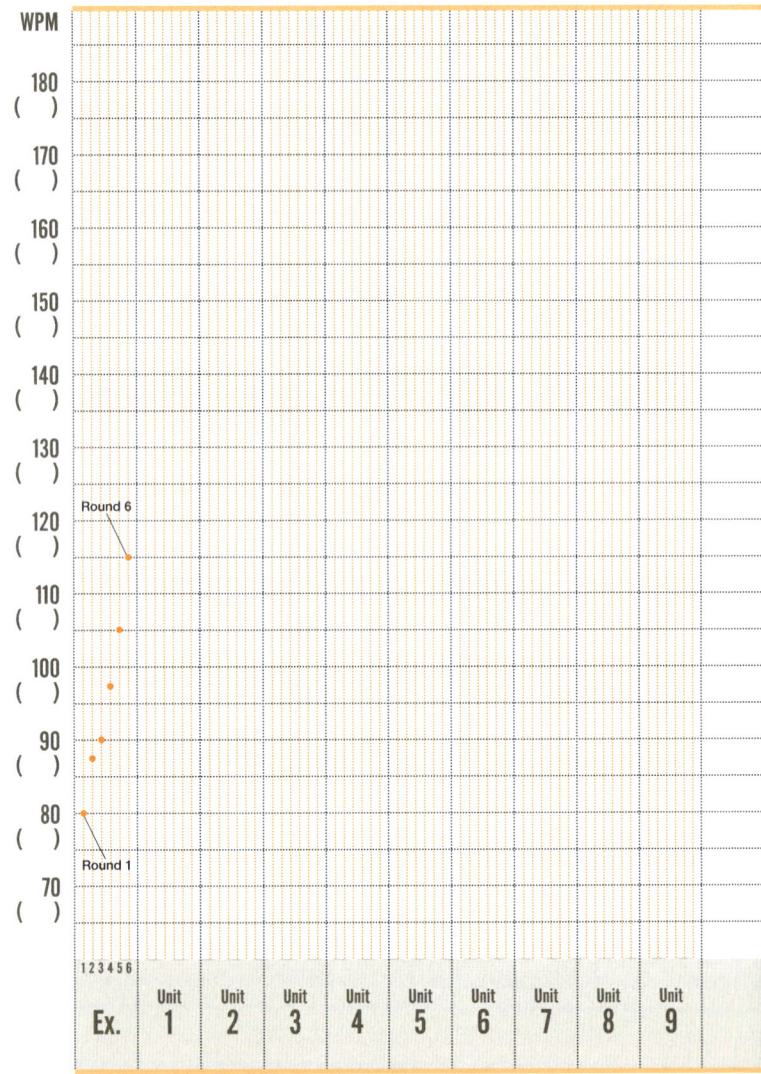

| Unit 10 | Unit 11 | Unit 12 | Unit 13 | Unit 14 | Unit 15 | Unit 16 | Unit 17 | Unit 18 | Unit 19 | Unit 20 |

WPM換算表

seconds	words per minute								
30	596	612	624	612	618	626	624	630	642
40	447	459	468	459	464	470	468	473	482
50	358	367	374	367	371	376	374	378	385
60	298	306	312	306	309	313	312	315	321
65	275	282	288	282	285	289	288	291	296
70	255	262	267	262	265	268	267	270	275
75	238	245	250	245	247	250	250	252	257
80	224	230	234	230	232	235	234	236	241
85	210	216	220	216	218	221	220	222	227
90	199	204	208	204	206	209	208	210	214
95	188	193	197	193	195	198	197	199	203
100	179	184	187	184	185	188	187	189	193
110	163	167	170	167	169	171	170	172	175
120	149	153	156	153	155	157	156	158	161
130	138	141	144	141	143	144	144	145	148
140	128	131	134	131	132	134	134	135	138
150	119	122	125	122	124	125	125	126	128
160	112	115	117	115	116	117	117	118	120
170	105	108	110	108	109	110	110	111	113
180	99	102	104	102	103	104	104	105	107
190	94	97	99	97	98	99	99	99	101
200	89	92	94	92	93	94	94	95	96
210	85	87	89	87	88	89	89	90	92
220	81	83	85	83	84	85	85	86	88
230	78	80	81	80	81	82	81	82	84
	Unit 1	Unit 2	Unit 3	Unit 4	Unit 5	Unit 6	Unit 7	Unit 8	Unit 9

words per minute

652	666	664	666	684	672	698	710	698	704	726
489	500	498	500	513	504	524	533	524	528	545
391	400	398	400	410	403	419	426	419	422	436
326	333	332	333	342	336	349	355	349	352	363
301	307	306	307	316	310	322	328	322	325	335
279	285	285	285	293	288	299	304	299	302	311
261	266	266	266	274	269	279	284	279	282	290
245	250	249	255	257	252	262	266	262	264	272
230	235	234	235	241	237	246	251	246	248	256
217	222	221	222	228	224	233	237	233	235	242
206	210	210	210	216	212	220	224	220	222	229
196	200	199	200	205	202	209	213	209	211	218
178	182	181	182	187	183	190	194	190	192	198
163	167	166	167	171	168	175	178	175	176	182
150	154	153	154	158	155	161	164	161	162	168
140	143	142	143	147	144	150	152	150	151	156
130	133	133	133	137	134	140	142	140	141	145
122	125	125	125	128	126	131	133	131	132	136
115	118	117	118	121	119	123	125	123	124	128
109	111	111	111	114	112	116	118	116	117	121
103	105	105	105	108	106	110	112	110	111	115
98	100	100	100	103	101	105	107	105	106	109
93	95	95	95	98	96	100	101	100	101	104
89	91	91	91	93	92	95	97	95	96	99
85	87	87	87	89	88	91	93	91	92	95
Unit 10	Unit 11	Unit 12	Unit 13	Unit 14	Unit 15	Unit 16	Unit 17	Unit 18	Unit 19	Unit 20

朗読音声について

本書の朗読音声))) は、
下記 URL から自由にダウンロードできます。

検索方法
朗日新聞出版 🔍
↓
朝日新聞出版ホームページのトップページ右上の
検索欄に「毎日の英速読」と入力してください
↓
「毎日の英速読」のページから、
パソコンで音声データをダウンロードしてください

URL：
http://publications.asahi.com/ecs/
detail/?item_id=15998

＊音声ダウンロードは、パソコン回線で行ってください。
スマートフォンや MP3 プレーヤーでご使用の場合は、
パソコンにダウンロードしたデータを転送してください。

速読トレーニング

UNIT別 Word数 一覧

UNIT 1	298 words
UNIT 2	306 words
UNIT 3	312 words
UNIT 4	306 words
UNIT 5	309 words
UNIT 6	313 words
UNIT 7	312 words
UNIT 8	315 words
UNIT 9	321 words
UNIT 10	326 words
UNIT 11	333 words
UNIT 12	332 words
UNIT 13	333 words
UNIT 14	342 words
UNIT 15	336 words
UNIT 16	349 words
UNIT 17	355 words
UNIT 18	349 words
UNIT 19	352 words
UNIT 20	363 words

Unit 01

Learning from the Bears
― フランス農民は「冬眠」していた？ ―

the French Revolution	フランス革命	instead of ~		～の代わりに
prevent	動 防ぐ	throughout ~	前	～を通してずっと
hunger	名 飢え	iron	名	鉄
gather	動 集まる	supplies	名	生活必需品
lie down	横たわる [過去形 lay / 過去分詞 lain]	exchange	動	交換する
take turns	順番に行う	explain	動	説明する
hibernate	動 冬眠する	industry	名	産業
sensible	形 理にかなっている	work on ~		～に取り組む
decision	名 決定	tiny	形	小さな
as long as possible	できるだけ長く	mechanism	名	装置

01 速読

Learning from Bears

French workers enjoy a standard 35-hour workweek. They like having more time to spend with their families. But is a short workweek good for the country? Does it result in more jobs for the nation's workers?

After the French Revolution, local leaders went out into the country and saw how people lived. They were surprised that most farmers did not work in the fields between autumn and spring. The farmers stayed in their homes and spent the cold months doing almost nothing. After working hard during the five months of warm weather, they were resting. By resting, they were preventing hunger.

The whole family gathered around a warm stove, lay down and went to sleep. Once a day everyone got up to eat a piece of hard bread. Then they went back to sleep. The members of the family took turns keeping the fire burning.

This was not "hibernating" like what bears do in the winter. But it was a sensible decision by the members of the family. Just stay in bed for as long as possible, and do no work. To these French farmers "working more to

Round 1	Round 2	Round 3	Round 4	Round 5	Round 6
WPM 語	WPM 語	WPM 語	WPM 語	WPM 語	WPM 語
月 日	月 日	月 日	月 日	月 日	月 日

earn more" did not seem like a good idea. Instead of working throughout the year, the people of one village on the Rhone River made enough money for one year at their summer fair. They spent the rest of the year relaxing, hunting and sleeping.

Few people needed money until the 20th century. They needed money for salt and iron. But they got most other supplies through exchanging goods. There wasn't a great need to make money. This helps explain why one of the winter industries in the high mountains was clock-making. Spending long hours working on tiny mechanisms was a way to make time pass faster.

298 words

01 True or False?

次の1〜6の文を読み、本文の内容に合っていたらT、合わなかったらF、述べられていなかったらNS（Not stated）を選んでください。

1	All workers in France work more than 35 hours per week.	T ☐ F ☐ NS ☐
2	French workers now work less than any other country.	T ☐ F ☐ NS ☐
3	Long ago, farmers rested during the winter.	T ☐ F ☐ NS ☐
4	Hibernating is something that bears do.	T ☐ F ☐ NS ☐
5	The people living near the Rhone River earned money in summer.	T ☐ F ☐ NS ☐
6	Clock-making was common during the summer months.	T ☐ F ☐ NS ☐

スラッシュ訳

Learning from Bears
熊から学ぶ

French workers enjoy / a standard 35-hour
（フランスの労働者は享受する／標準的な週35時間労働を）
workweek. // They like / having more time / to spend
（彼らは好む／より多くの時間を持つことを／家族と過ごす）
with their families. // But is a short workweek good /
（しかし週間の労働時間が短いことは良いか）
for the country? // Does it result in more jobs / for the
（国にとって／それはより多くの雇用機会をもたらすか／国の）
nation's workers? //
（労働者にとって）

After the French Revolution, / local leaders went
（フランス革命の後／地域の指導者は田舎に行った）
out into the country / and saw / how people lived. //
（そして見た／どのように人々が生活しているかを）
They were surprised / that most farmers did not
（彼らは驚いた／農民のほとんどが働かないことに）
work / in the fields / between autumn and spring. //
（畑で／秋から春の間）
The farmers stayed in their homes / and spent the
（農民は家にとどまっていた／そして寒い月を過ごした）
cold months / doing almost nothing. // After working
（ほとんど何もしないで／一生懸命働いた後）
hard / during the five months of warm weather, / they
（5カ月の気候の暖かい間／彼ら）
were resting. // By resting, / they were preventing
（は休んでいた／休むことによって／彼らは飢えを防いでいた）
hunger. //

01 スラッシュ訳

The whole family gathered / around a warm stove, / lay down / and went to sleep. // Once a day / everyone got up / to eat a piece of hard bread. // Then they went back to sleep. // The members of the family took turns / keeping the fire burning. //

This was not "hibernating" / like what bears do in the winter. // But it was a sensible decision / by the members of the family. // Just stay in bed / for as long as possible, / and do no work. // To these French farmers / "working more to earn more" / did not seem like a good idea. // Instead of working throughout the year, / the people of one village on the Rhone River / made enough money for one year / at their summer fair. // They spent the rest of the year / relaxing, hunting and sleeping. //

Few people needed money / until the 20th century. //

彼らはお金が必要だった / 塩と鉄を買うために // しかし彼らはそれ
They needed money / for salt and iron. // But they got
以外のほとんどの必需品を得た / 商品の交換によって
most other supplies / through exchanging goods /
大した必要性がなかった / お金を稼ぐ // これは説
There wasn't a great need / to make money. // This
明するのを助ける / なぜ冬期の産業のひとつが
helps explain / why one of the winter industries / in
高い山で / 時計作りだった // 長い時間を
the high mountains / was clock-making. // Spending
費やすことは / 小さな装置に作業を行って / ひとつの方法で
long hours / working on tiny mechanisms / was a
あった / 時間が経つのを早くする //
way / to make time pass faster. //

01　和訳 & 解答

熊から学ぶ

　フランスの労働者は、週35時間労働制を享受している。彼らは家族とともに過ごす時間が長いほうがよいのだ。しかし、週ごとの労働時間が短いのは、国にとっては良いことだろうか。国の労働者にとっては雇用機会の増加をもたらすのだろうか。

　フランス革命後、地域の指導者らが田舎におもむいて人々の生活を見てみたところ、驚いたことに農民のほとんどが秋から春の間は畑に働きに出ていなかった。その寒い数カ月間は家から出ず、ほとんど何もせずに過ごしていた。気候の暖かい5カ月間は懸命に働き、その後は休息していた。休息することで、飢えを防いでいたのだ。

　一家みんなで暖かいストーブを囲んで横になって眠った。全員が一日に一度、堅いパンを食べるために起きて、その後は再び眠る。家族が交代で火をたやさないようにした。

　これは熊が冬にする「冬眠」ではない。しかし、家族にとっては賢明な判断だった。できる限りベッドから出ず、仕事もしない。これらフランスの農民には、「もっと働き、もっと稼ごう」は好ましい選択ではなかったようだ。ローヌ川沿いのある村の人々は、1年を通して働く代わりに、夏の市で1年分のお金を稼ぎ、年の残りはただくつろいだり、狩りをしたり、眠ったりして過ごした。

　20世紀に入るまでは、ほとんどの人々にとってお金は必要ではなかった。塩と鉄はお金で買わなくてはならなかったが、他の必需品のほとんどは、物々交換で入手できた。お金を稼ぐ必要に迫られていなかったのだ。これは、高山での冬期産業のひとつが時計の製造であることのひとつの説明になる。長い時間をかけて小さな装置に取り組めば、時間が早く過ぎるのだ。

True or False　解答 & 和訳

1. F　全てのフランスの労働者は、週に35時間以上働く。
2. NS　フランスの労働者は、他のどの国の労働者より働く時間が少ない。
3. T　大昔、農民は冬の間休んでいた。
4. T　冬眠は熊がするものだ。
5. T　ローヌ川の近くに住んでいた人々は夏に収入を得た。
6. F　時計づくりは、夏の間によく行われた。

Unit 02

Juan the Bear
― 檻の中の動物たち ―

reproduce	動 再現する	before long	間もなく
environment	名 環境	whether	接 ～かどうか
shelter	名 隠れ場	appear	動 現れる
enemy	名 敵	point of view	視点
necessity	名 必要品	moat	名 堀
numerous	形 たくさんの	succeed	動 成功する
zebra	名 シマウマ	smart	形 利口な
nearby	形 近くの	habitat	名 生活場所
exhibit	名 展示	tranquilize	動 [麻酔によって]鎮静させる
completely	副 完全に	official	名 職員

Juan the Bear

Since the 1970s and 1980s, zoos around the world have tried to reproduce the natural environment of their animals. They have taken out hard concrete floors and steel bars. They have put in grass, trees, and pools of water. These environments seem more natural to humans, but what about the animals? It is true that the animals do not have to worry about finding food, shelter, or safety from enemies. All the necessities of life seem to be provided for them. While this may not seem like such a bad deal, the animals experience numerous problems.

The zebras, for example, live in fear. They can smell the lions in the nearby Great Cats exhibit every day and they are completely unable to escape. There is no possibility of moving to a safer place. Moreover, zoo animals cannot gather food for the winter. This must make the birds and animals feel they will die before long. They get food today. But they have no way of knowing whether food will appear again tomorrow. They have no way to get food for themselves. In short, zoo life is completely unnatural from the animals' point of view.

Animals in zoos have almost no control over their own lives. In spite of the efforts of their human caretakers, animals in zoos may feel caught in a death trap. They are surrounded by walls, nets, moats and glass. Every year some animals try to escape. Some of them succeed. In 2004, at the Berlin zoo, there was a bear named Juan. This smart bear rode on a log across the moat surrounding his habitat. He then climbed a wall to freedom. He took a ride on the zoo's merry-go-round. He enjoyed going down the slide. But eventually he was tranquilized by zoo officials and returned to his habitat.

306 words

02 True or False?

次の1~6の文を読み、本文の内容に合っていたらT、合わなかったらF、述べられていなかったらNS (Not stated) を選んでください。

1	Zoos have replaced grass and trees with concrete.	T ☐ F ☐ NS ☐
2	The smell of lions gives zebras fear.	T ☐ F ☐ NS ☐
3	Animals in zoos feel safe from other animals.	T ☐ F ☐ NS ☐
4	Animals are sure they will receive food every day.	T ☐ F ☐ NS ☐
5	Juan was the only bear in the Berlin zoo.	T ☐ F ☐ NS ☐
6	After escaping from his habitat, Juan was not found again.	T ☐ F ☐ NS ☐

スラッシュ訳

file-04

熊のフアン
Juan the Bear

Since the 1970s and 1980s, / zoos around the world have tried / to reproduce / the natural environment / of their animals. // They have taken out / hard concrete floors and steel bars. // They have put in / grass, trees, and pools of water. // These environments seem more natural / to humans, / but what about the animals? // It is true / that the animals do not have to worry / about finding food, shelter, or safety from enemies. // All the necessities of life / seem to be provided for them. // While this may not seem like / such a bad deal, / the animals experience numerous problems. //

The zebras, for example, live in fear. // They can smell the lions / in the nearby Great Cats exhibit /

02 スラッシュ訳

毎日 / そして彼らは全くできない / 逃げることが
every day / and they are completely unable / to escape. //
可能性がない / より安全な場所に移る
There is no possibility / of moving to a safer place. //
その上 / 動物園の動物は食料を集めることができない / 冬に備えて
Moreover, / zoo animals cannot gather food / for the
　　　　それは鳥や動物に感じさせるに違いない
winter. // This must make the birds and animals feel /
彼らは間もなく死ぬであろう // 彼らは今日餌を得る // しかし
they will die before long. // They get food today. // But
彼らには知る方法がない / 餌が明日再び現れるかどうか
they have no way of knowing / whether food will appear
　　　　　　　　// 彼らは方法を持っていない / 自分で食料を得る
again tomorrow. // They have no way / to get food for
　　　　　　　// 簡単に言って / 動物園での暮らしは完全に不自然である
themselves. // In short, / zoo life is completely unnatural
/ 動物の視点からは
/ from the animals' point of view. //
　　　動物園の動物はほとんどコントロールすることができない / 彼ら自身の
Animals in zoos have almost no control / over their
生活を // 人間の飼育係の努力にもかかわらず
own lives. // In spite of the efforts of their human
　　　　　　/ 動物園の動物は感じているかもしれない / 死のわなに捉えられて
caretakers, / animals in zoos may feel / caught in a
いると // 彼らは囲まれている / 壁や網や堀やガラスによっ
death trap. // They are surrounded / by walls, nets,
て　　　　　　　　// 毎年、何頭かの動物が脱走を試みる
moats and glass. // Every year some animals try to
　　　　　// そのうち何頭かは成功する // 2004年ベルリン動物園に
escape. // Some of them succeed. // In 2004, at the
　　　　　　　/ フアンという名前の熊がいた
Berlin zoo, / there was a bear named Juan. // This

smart bear rode on a log / across the moat surrounding his habitat. // He then climbed a wall / to freedom. // He took a ride on the zoo's merry-go-round. // He enjoyed going down the slide. // But eventually / he was tranquilized // by zoo officials / and returned to his habitat. //

02 和訳 & 解答

熊のフアン

　1970～1980年代から、世界中の動物園は、動物の本来の自然環境を再現しようと努めてきた。堅いコンクリートの床と鉄鋼の檻を撤去し、草木や池を取り入れた。こういった環境は、人間にはより自然なように見えるが、動物にとってはどうだろう。たしかに、動物たちは食べ物や隠れる場所や敵からの避難場所を探す心配をしなくてよい。生きるのに必要なものはすべて用意されているように見える。それほど悪い取引ではないように見えるものの、動物たちは多くの問題に悩まされている。

　たとえばシマウマは怯えて暮らしている。すぐ近くのネコ科大型動物の展示にライオンがいるのが臭いでわかるのに、逃げる手段を断たれている。より安全な場所へ移動することが不可能なのだ。そのうえ、動物園の動物は冬に備えて食べ物を集めることができない。こうなると鳥や動物は、長くは生きられないと感じるだろう。今日は食べ物を得られたが、明日も得られるかどうかを知るすべがない。自分で食べ物を得る手段がないのだ。つまり動物の観点からすれば、動物園での生活は全く不自然である。

　動物園にいる動物は、自分の生活を全くコントロールできない。人間の飼育係の努力にもかかわらず、動物園の動物たちは、死のわなにかかったように感じているかもしれない。動物たちは、壁や網や堀やガラスによって囲まれている。毎年、脱走を試みる動物たちがおり、成功する場合もある。2004年に、ベルリン動物園にフアンという名前のクマがいた。この利口なクマは居住区域を囲む堀を丸太に乗って渡り、壁をよじ登って逃げ出した。動物園のメリーゴーランドに乗り、すべり台を下るのを楽しんだ。しかし最後は動物園の職員によって麻酔を打たれ、居住区域に戻された。

True or False 解答 & 和訳

1. F　動物園は草や木々をコンクリートに置き換えた。
2. T　ライオンの匂いがシマウマを脅えさせる。
3. F　動物園の動物たちは、他の動物（の脅威）から安全だと感じている。
4. F　動物たちは、毎日餌を得られると確信している。
5. NS　フアンは、そのベルリン動物園でたった一頭の熊だった。
6. F　フアンは、彼の居住地域から逃げたあと、再び見つけられることはなかった。

Unit 03

GDP Man
— 働いて稼ぎまくるか、ゆったり暮らすか —

progress	名 進歩	transportation	名 交通
measure	動 測定する	take care of ~	~の面倒をみる
statistic	名 統計	too busy to ~	忙しすぎて~できない
gross	名 総計	in contrast	対照的に
domestic	形 国内の	grow	動 栽培する
product	名 生産量	exercise	動 運動する
goods	名 商品	rather than ~	~するのではなく
necessarily	副 必ずしも	in terms of ~	~に関して
compare	動 較べる	better off	暮らしがより良い状態にある
commute	名 通勤	quality	名 質

GDP Man

Each of us has an idea of what progress looks like. For some of us, it is a new place to live. For others, it is a new television or a trip abroad. For most governments around the world, however, progress is measured by just one statistic: gross domestic product, or GDP.

GDP includes how many goods companies produce, how much food farmers produce, and how many new buildings builders put up. As a country's GDP rises, some people think, the lifestyle of the people gets better. But not everyone agrees with this way of thinking. A higher GDP does not necessarily mean that the people of a country are happier or enjoying life more. A new, different way of measuring progress compares two categories of people: High-GDP Man and Low-GDP Man.

High-GDP Man has a long commute to work. He spends a lot of money on transportation between his home and his office. The stresses of his commute are not good for his heart or for his car if he drives. He works hard, spends a lot, and often goes to bars and restaurants. He and his wife both work, so they have to

Round 1	Round 2	Round 3	Round 4	Round 5	Round 6
WPM　語	WPM　語	WPM　語	WPM　語	WPM　語	WPM　語
月　日	月　日	月　日	月　日	月　日	月　日

find someone to take care of their children. He and his wife are usually too busy to take long vacations.

In contrast, Low-GDP Man spends a lot of time cooking, cleaning, and taking care of his house. He grows some of his own vegetables. He borrows books from his local library instead of buying them. He eats at home and spends more time with his family. He exercises by doing housework, rather than paying to belong to a gym.

In terms of economic measures, High-GDP Man is better off. But we cannot really be sure whether his life is any better. In terms of quality of life, Low-GDP Man may be both happier and healthier.

312 words

03 True or False?

次の1〜6の文を読み、本文の内容に合っていたらT、合わなかったらF、述べられていなかったらNS（Not stated）を選んでください。

1	Each of us has a different view of progress.	T ☐ F ☐ NS ☐
2	Many governments think of progress as having a new place to live.	T ☐ F ☐ NS ☐
3	People with high incomes enjoy their lives more than others.	T ☐ F ☐ NS ☐
4	Commuting is stressful for Low-GDP Man.	T ☐ F ☐ NS ☐
5	Low-GDP Man usually eats at home rather than going to restaurants.	T ☐ F ☐ NS ☐
6	GDP doesn't tell us whether people are happier or healthier.	T ☐ F ☐ NS ☐

スラッシュ訳

file-06

GDP マン
GDP Man

Each of us has an idea / of what progress looks like. // For some of us, / it is a new place to live. // For others, / it is a new television / or a trip abroad. // For most governments around the world, / however, / progress is measured / by just one statistic: / gross domestic product, or GDP. //

GDP includes / how many goods companies produce, / how much food farmers produce, / and how many new buildings builders put up. // As a country's GDP rises, / some people think, / the lifestyle of the people gets better. // But not everyone agrees with this way of thinking. // A higher GDP does not necessarily mean / that the people of a country are happier / or enjoying life more. // A new, different

03 スラッシュ訳

way of measuring progress / compares / two
　　別の方法は　　　　　　　　　　　較べる

categories of people: / High-GDP Man and Low-GDP
　2つの種類の人々を　　　　高GDP人間と低GDP人間

Man. //

　High-GDP Man has a long commute / to work. // He
　　高GDP人間は通勤時間が長い　　　　　　職場まで

spends a lot of money / on transportation / between
　彼はたくさんのお金を使う　　交通に

his home and his office. // The stresses of his commute
　家とオフィスの間の　　　　　通勤のストレスは良くない

are not good / for his heart / or for his car / if he
　　　　　　　彼の心臓にとって　または彼の車に　もし彼が

drives. // He works hard, / spends a lot, / and often
車を運転するなら　彼は一生懸命働く　お金をたくさん使う　そしてバーや

goes to bars and restaurants. // He and his wife both
　レストランによく行く　　　　　　　彼と彼の妻は共に働く

work, / so they have to find someone / to take care of
　　　　なので、彼らは誰かを見つけなければならない　子供の面倒をみる

their children. // He and his wife are usually too busy /
　　　　　　　　彼と彼の妻はいつも、忙しすぎる

to take long vacations. //
長い休暇を取るには

　In contrast, / Low-GDP Man spends a lot of time /
　　対照的に　　　低GDP人間は多くの時間を費やす

cooking, cleaning, and taking care of his house. // He
料理をしたり、掃除をしたり、家の手入れをするのに　　　　彼は

grows some of his own vegetables. // He borrows
　自分自身の野菜を育てる　　　　　　　彼は地元の

books from his local library / instead of buying them. //
　図書館から本を借りる　　　　買う代わりに

彼は家で食事をする / そして家族と多くの時間を過ごす
He eats at home / and spends more time with his family. // 彼は家事をすることで運動をする
He exercises by doing housework, / rather
お金を払ってジムに加入するのではなく
than paying to belong to a gym. //

経済指標の観点から / 高GDP人間は暮らしが
In terms of economic measures, / High-GDP Man
より良い状態にある // しかし我々は本当に確信を持つことはできない // 彼の人生が
is better off. // But we cannot really be sure // whether
より良いものかどうか // 生活の質の観点から
his life is any better. // In terms of quality of life, /
低GDP人間の方がより幸せで健康的かもしれない
Low-GDP Man may be both happier and healthier. //

03 和訳＆解答

GDP マン

　我々はそれぞれ進歩がどういうものであるかということに関して異なる考えを持っている。人によってそれは新居であったり、または新しいテレビや海外旅行だったりする。だが、世界中のほとんどの政府にとって、進歩はただひとつの統計によって測定される。国内総生産、すなわちGDPだ。

　GDPには、企業がどれだけの商品を製造し、農家がどれだけの食物を生産し、そして建築業者がどれだけの新しい建物を建設するかが含まれる。国のGDPが成長するのに伴い、人々の生活も向上すると考える人もいる。しかし、誰もがこの考え方に同感というわけではない。GDPが、国民がより幸せで人生をより楽しんでいることの証しとは限らない。進歩を測る新たな別の方法では、2つのカテゴリーの人々を比較する。高GDP人間と低GDP人間だ。

　高GDP人間は通勤時間が長く、自宅とオフィスの間の移動に多くのお金を使う。通勤のストレスは心臓に負担になるし、もし運転するなら車にも負担をかける。よく働き、出費が多く、バーやレストランによく行く。妻とは共稼ぎなので、子供の世話は誰かに頼まなければならない。夫婦のどちらも、大抵は忙しすぎて長期休暇も取れない。

　これとは対照的に、低GDP人間は、料理や掃除や家の手入れに多くの時間をかける。自分で野菜を育てる。本は買わずに地元の図書館から借りる。食事は自宅でとり、家族とともに過ごす時間が長い。彼は有料のジムに通う代わりに、家事をすることで運動する。

　経済指標の観点から、高GDP人間のほうが暮らし向きは良い。しかし、それがより良い人生かどうかは疑問である。人生の質という観点からすると、低GDP人間のほうが健康で幸福かもしれない。

True or False　解答＆和訳

1. T　我々はそれぞれ、進歩に対する違った見方を持っている。
2. F　多くの政府は、進歩を新しい住居を得ることだと考えている。
3. NS　収入の多い人たちは、そうではない人々より生活を楽しんでいる。
4. NS　通勤は低GDP人間にとってストレスになる。
5. T　低GDP人間は、たいていレストランに行くよりも家で食事をする。
6. T　GDPは、人々がより幸福であるか、健康であるかを教えてはくれない。

Unit 04

The Camera Thief
— ワニとウミワシとカメラ泥棒 —

thief	名 泥棒	occasion	名 場合
researcher	名 研究者	on several occasions	何度か
record	動 記録する	scenery	名 景色
crocodile	名 ワニ	examine	動 調べる
set up	設置する	discover	動 理解する
edge	名 端	grab	動 掴む
motion sensor	運動センサー	take off	飛び立つ
turn on	スイッチが入る	sea eagle	ウミワシ
disappear	動 消える	mystery	名 謎
wash away	流す	soften	動 やわらかくする
hardly	副 ほとんど〜できない	pick at ~	〜をつつく

04 速読

The Camera Thief

A group of researchers wanted to record the movements of crocodiles in a river in Australia. To do this, they set up a small video camera along the edge of the river. It had a small motion sensor. When something moved in front of the lens, the video turned on.

When the researchers later went to check on the camera, however, the camera had disappeared. They guessed that it had fallen into the water and been washed away.

After several months, someone found the camera—110 kilometers away—and returned it to the research group. The researchers decided to look at the video. They were able to see three 30-second sections. They could hardly believe their eyes. On several occasions, one of their cameras had been moved by a wild animal. But this time was different. The film showed interesting scenery from high in the sky.

After examining the film, the group discovered how the camera had disappeared. They also found out who the "thief" was. The film showed the wings of a bird as it grabbed the camera and took off. It showed short views

Round 1	Round 2	Round 3	Round 4	Round 5	Round 6
WPM 語	WPM 語	WPM 語	WPM 語	WPM 語	WPM 語
月 日	月 日	月 日	月 日	月 日	月 日

of the land and the sky during its long journey. And then it showed the thief. It was a sea eagle.

But there was another mystery. Why did the sea eagle carry the camera for such a long distance? Sea eagles usually take what they catch, fly up into the sky, and drop it. Dropping it to the ground softens it and makes it easier to eat. The research group guessed that this bird was young and still learning how to do things. It "caught" the camera and carried it away but didn't drop it. When it put the camera down, it started picking at it. When it did, it took a picture of itself.

306 words

04 True or False?

次の 1 〜 6 の文を読み、本文の内容に合っていたら T、合わなかったら F、述べられていなかったら NS（Not stated）を選んでください。

1. The camera was found in the north-west of Australia.
   - T ☐
   - F ☐
   - NS ☐

2. Researchers at first thought a crocodile had eaten the camera.
   - T ☐
   - F ☐
   - NS ☐

3. The research group could not see any visual images when it was found.
   - T ☐
   - F ☐
   - NS ☐

4. The thief carried the camera on land for 110 kilometers.
   - T ☐
   - F ☐
   - NS ☐

5. Sea eagles usually drop what they catch from the sky to the ground.
   - T ☐
   - F ☐
   - NS ☐

6. Only the wings of the bird appeared in the film.
   - T ☐
   - F ☐
   - NS ☐

スラッシュ訳

file-08

カメラ泥棒
The Camera Thief

研究者のグループは記録したかった
A group of researchers wanted to record / the
ワニの移動を / オーストラリアの川で
movements of crocodiles / in a river in Australia. // To
それをするために / 彼らは小さいビデオカメラを設置した / 川の端に
do this, / they set up a small video camera / along
それは小さな運動センサーが付いていた
the edge of the river. // It had a small motion sensor. //
何かが動くとき / レンズの前で
When something moved / in front of the lens, / the
ビデオが作動した
video turned on. //

研究者が後で行ったとき / カメラを確認するため
When the researchers later went / to check on the
に / しかし / カメラは消えていた
camera, / however, / the camera had disappeared. //
彼らは推測した / それは水に落ちた
They guessed / that it had fallen into the water / and
そして流された
been washed away. //

数カ月後 / 誰かがカメラを見つけた
After several months, / someone found the camera
/ 110キロ離れたところで / そして返した / 研究
/ —110 kilometers away— / and returned it / to the
グループに / 研究者は決めた / ビデオを
research group. // The researchers decided / to look
見ることに / 彼らは見ることができた
at the video. // They were able to see / three

04 スラッシュ訳

30-second sections. // They could hardly believe their eyes. // On several occasions, / one of their cameras had been moved / by a wild animal. // But this time was different. // The film showed interesting scenery / from high in the sky. //

After examining the film, / the group discovered / how the camera had disappeared. // They also found out / who the "thief" was. // The film showed the wings of a bird / as it grabbed the camera / and took off. // It showed short views / of the land and the sky / during its long journey. // And then it showed the thief. // It was a sea eagle. /

But there was another mystery. // Why did the sea eagle carry the camera / for such a long distance? // Sea eagles usually take what they catch, / fly up into the sky, / and drop it. // Dropping it to the ground /

softens it / and makes it easier to eat. // The research group guessed / that this bird was young / and still learning / how to do things. // It "caught" the camera / and carried it away / but didn't drop it. // When it put the camera down, / it started picking at it. // When it did, / it took a picture of itself. //

04 和訳 & 解答

カメラ泥棒

　ある研究者のグループが、オーストラリアの川でワニの動きを録画しようとした。そのため彼らは、川の端に小型ビデオカメラを設置した。それには小型運動感知センサーがついていて、レンズの前で何かが動くとビデオが作動するようになっていた。

　しかし、後で研究者がカメラをチェックしに行くと、カメラは消えていた。彼らは、カメラが水に落ちて流されたのだと思った。

　数カ月後、カメラが見つかった―110キロ離れたところで―そして研究グループに返された。彼らはビデオを見てみることにした。30秒の映像が3つ映し出されたが、目を疑うような内容だった。それまでにも、カメラが野生動物によって動かされたことは何度かあったが、しかし今回は異なっていた。映像には、はるか上空からの興味深い景色が映っていたのだ。

　映像を調べた後、グループはカメラがどのようになくなったかを知った。そして、「泥棒」の正体もわかった。映像には、カメラをつかんで飛び去る鳥の翼が映っていたのだ。映像には、長旅の間の地面と空が短く映し出され、その後に泥棒が映った。それは、ウミワシだった。

　しかし、謎はもう一つあった。なぜウミワシはそれほど遠くまでカメラを運んだのだろうか。ウミワシは通常、捕えた獲物を上空へ持って行って、上から落とす。地面に落とすことで柔らかくして、食べやすくするのだ。研究者グループは、このウミワシが若鳥で、まだやり方を学んでいるところだったのだろうと考えた。ウミワシはカメラを「捕獲して」、持ち去ったが、地面には落とさなかった。カメラを置いた後につつき始め、その時に自らの写真を撮ったのだ。

True or False　解答 & 和訳

1. NS　そのカメラは、オーストラリアの北西で見つかった。
2. F　研究者は、最初、ワニがカメラを食べてしまったと考えた。
3. F　研究グループは、それが見つかったとき、どんな画像も見られなかった。
4. F　その泥棒は、そのカメラを陸路で110キロも運んだ。
5. T　ウミワシは、通常、捕まえたものを空から陸地に向かって落とす。
6. F　そのフィルムにはその鳥の翼だけが写っていた。

Unit 05

The New Breadwinner
— 現代アメリカ家庭の大黒柱は? —

breadwinner	名 稼ぎ手	surprising	形 驚くべき
increasingly	副 ますます	graduate	動 卒業する
by choice	自ら選んで	workforce	名 労働人口
restructuring	名 リストラ	no longer	もはや〜でな
continuing	形 継続している	give way to ~	〜に取って代わられる
as a result	結果として	emphasize	動 強調する
when it comes to ~	〜のことになると	gender equality	男女平等
leading role	主導的な役割	bother	動 気にする
in other words	言い換えれば	helpless	形 無力な
entirely	副 完全に	ashamed	形 恥ずかしい

05 速読

The New Breadwinner

Until recently the husband was usually the breadwinner of the American family. But increasingly it is the wife who earns more than half of the income of a family. According to one study, in families in the top fifth of income categories, about 34% of the breadwinners are women. In the bottom fifth, however, close to 70% have women as the breadwinner. Not all of these women are "breadwinners" by choice. In many cases, restructuring and a continuing poor economy have taken jobs from men. As a result, women have had to go to work in order to support their families.

These women breadwinners are likely to keep separate bank accounts. They also have a bank account that their husbands do not know about. But when it comes to making decisions, many women let their husband take the leading role. In other words, they try to support the image of the strong husband.

The change in who is the breadwinner is not entirely surprising. For one thing, these days more than half of those who graduate from college are women. Second, women now make up 50% of the workforce. Third, close to 40% of women in the workforce were never married or are no longer married. It is only natural that they are breadwinners.

  Is this the end of men as the stronger half of the family? Are strong males giving way to strong females? Most American men who are now working were raised in the generation after the women's movement. They grew up in a culture that emphasized the values of gender equality. It doesn't bother them that their wives earn more income. But many men still want their own salary to be enough to support their family. These men may feel helpless. They may even feel ashamed that they are not the main breadwinner.

309 words

05 True or False?

次の1〜6の文を読み、本文の内容に合っていたらT、合わなかったらF、述べられていなかったらNS（Not stated）を選んでください。

---

1. American wives were the breadwinners in the past.

   T ☐
   F ☐
   NS ☐

2. Wives are happy to become breadwinners.

   T ☐
   F ☐
   NS ☐

3. Some women breadwinners keep separate bank accounts.

   T ☐
   F ☐
   NS ☐

4. Fifty percent or more of recent graduates of college are women.

   T ☐
   F ☐
   NS ☐

5. More than one third of working women do not have husbands.

   T ☐
   F ☐
   NS ☐

6. Some men still want to earn enough money to support their families.

   T ☐
   F ☐
   NS ☐

スラッシュ訳

file-10

新たな稼ぎ頭
The New Breadwinner

Until recently / the husband was usually the breadwinner / of the American family. // But increasingly / it is the wife / who earns more than half / of the income / of a family. // According to one study, / in families / in the top fifth of income categories, / about 34% of the breadwinners are women. // In the bottom fifth, / however, / close to 70% have women as the breadwinner. // Not all of these women are "breadwinners" / by choice. // In many cases, / restructuring and a continuing poor economy / have taken jobs from men. // As a result, / women have had to go to work / in order to support their families. //

These women breadwinners are likely / to keep

05 スラッシュ訳

separate bank accounts. // They also have a bank account / that their husbands do not know about. // But when it comes to making decisions, / many women let their husband take the leading role. // In other words, / they try to support the image of the strong husband. // The change in who is the breadwinner / is not entirely surprising. // For one thing, / these days more than half of those / who graduate from college / are women. // Second, / women now make up 50% of the workforce. // Third, / close to 40% of women / in the workforce / were never married / or are no longer married. // It is only natural / that they are breadwinners. //

Is this the end of men / as the stronger half of the family? // Are strong males giving way / to strong females? // Most American men / who are now working / were raised in the generation / after the women's movement. // They grew up in a culture / that emphasized the values of gender equality. // It doesn't bother them / that their wives earn more income. // But many men still want / their own salary to be enough / to support their family. // These men may feel helpless. // They may even feel ashamed / that they are not the main breadwinner. //

05 和訳 & 解答

新たな稼ぎ手

　つい最近まで、アメリカでは普通、夫が一家の稼ぎ手だった。しかし現在では、家族の収入の大半を妻が稼ぐ場合が増えつつある。ある調査によれば、収入の上位1/5に入る家庭では、稼ぎ手の約34％が女性だ。しかし、下位1/5の家庭では、稼ぎ手の約70％が女性である。これらの女性たちの全員が、自ら好んで「大黒柱」になっているわけではない。多くの場合、リストラと長引く不況で男性が失業した結果、女性が家族を養うために働きに出なければならなかったのだ。

　これら女性の稼ぎ手たちは、別の銀行口座を持つことが多い。夫の知らない銀行口座も持っている。しかし彼女らの多くは、意思決定に関しては夫に主導権を譲る。言い換えれば、強い夫というイメージを支えようとしているのだ。

　稼ぎ手の変遷は、それほど不思議なことではない。まずひとつには、最近では大学卒業者の過半数が女性である。次に、現在の労働人口の50％が女性である。さらに、働く女性の40％近くが未婚または離婚している。彼女たちが稼ぎ手であるのは極めて当然のことだ。

　男性が家庭内で強い地位を占める時代は終わったのだろうか。強い男性たちは、強い女性たちに取って代わられつつあるのか。現在職についているアメリカ人男性の大部分は、女性運動の後の世代に育てられた。男女平等の価値観を強調する文化の中で育ったのだ。彼らは妻のほうが多くの収入を得ても気にしない。しかし、いまだに多くの男性は、自分自身で家族を養うのに十分な収入を得ることを望んでいる。こういった男性は無力感をおぼえるかもしれないし、自分が大黒柱でないことは恥だとさえ思うかもしれない。

True or False　解答 & 和訳

1. F　アメリカの妻たちは、かつて稼ぎ手だった。
2. NS　妻たちは稼ぎ手になれて幸福だった。
3. T　女性の稼ぎ手には、別の銀行口座を持っている人もいる。
4. T　最近の大学卒業者の50％以上が女性である。
5. T　働く女性の3分の1以上は夫がいない。
6. T　まだ、家族を養うのに十分なお金を稼ぎたいと思っている男たちがいる。

Unit 06

Keeping an Eye on You
― 防犯カメラは何を見ているか? ―

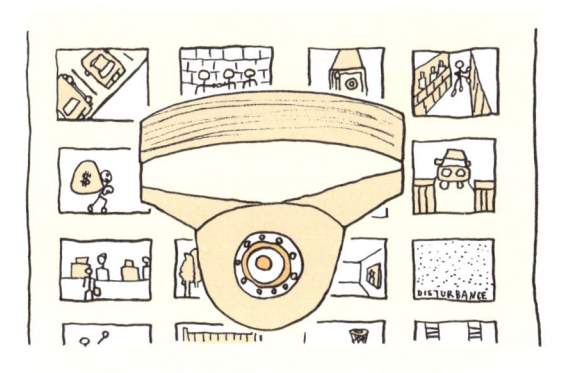

keep an eye on ~	～を見張る	observe	動 観察する
security camera	防犯カメラ	attract	動 引きつける
prevent	動 防ぐ	install	動 設置する
attempt	名 試み	note	動 記録する
serve	動 (目的を)果たす	gender	名 性別
serve	動 (客に)対応する	on the basis of ~	～に基づき
determine	動 割り出す	track	動 追跡する
ethnicity	名 人種	count	動 数える
notice	動 気づく	frequently	副 頻繁に
post	動 (人を)配置する	recognize	動 認識する

06 速読

Keeping an Eye on You

Everywhere we go, we are being watched. Security cameras record us in meeting rooms, restaurants, and subway stations. These cameras are set up to protect people and prevent crimes. In stores, cameras are used to prevent stealing and to record attempts to steal money from the cash register.

Now those same cameras are serving another purpose: they are watching how we shop. They record how many people enter a store each hour it is open. Managers can use this data to make staff schedules. When crowds come, the managers can be sure that there will be enough salespeople to serve them. Cameras in some shops are able to determine customers' ethnicity. Noticing that groups of tourists from one foreign country came in the shop at the same time every day, the manager posted sales staff who could speak their language.

Cameras also observe what products we look at and how we move through the store. Managers use this data to decide where to place goods on shelves and how to attract the customer's attention. Some stores

Round 1	Round 2	Round 3	Round 4	Round 5	Round 6
WPM 語	WPM 語	WPM 語	WPM 語	WPM 語	WPM 語
月 日	月 日	月 日	月 日	月 日	月 日

have installed widescreen monitors to show floor plans and advertisements for special sale items. Behind each monitor is a camera which notes eye movement. The camera tries to determine the viewer's gender and age group. On the basis of this data, the screen then changes to show advertisements for products that the person might like.

Recently some stores track signals from cell phones. They can find out how many people walking by their store actually come in. They can count how many minutes a person stays in the store, too. Although the store managers do not know who owns the phone, they do know how frequently the phone—and its owner—enters the store. In other words, they can recognize repeat customers. Shop managers find this information very helpful for their business.

313 words

06 True or False?

次の1～6の文を読み、本文の内容に合っていたらT、合わなかったらF、述べられていなかったらNS（Not stated）を選んでください。

1	Security cameras are used to prevent crime.	T ☐ / F ☐ / NS ☐
2	Camera data does not help managers run their business.	T ☐ / F ☐ / NS ☐
3	Show windows have cameras in them.	T ☐ / F ☐ / NS ☐
4	Widescreen monitors are sometimes used to show sale items.	T ☐ / F ☐ / NS ☐
5	Tracking signals from cell phones is against the law.	T ☐ / F ☐ / NS ☐
6	Shop managers know the names of cell phone owners.	T ☐ / F ☐ / NS ☐

スラッシュ訳

file-12

あなたを監視している
Keeping an Eye on You

我々が行く所はどこでも / 我々は見張られている
Everywhere we go, / we are being watched. //

防犯カメラは我々を録画する / 会議室、レストラン、
Security cameras record us / in meeting rooms,

そして地下鉄の駅で // これらのカメラは設置さ
restaurants, and subway stations. // These cameras

れている / 人々を守るために / そして犯罪を防ぐために //
are set up / to protect people / and prevent crimes. //

店内では / カメラは窃盗を防ぐために使われている /
In stores, / cameras are used to prevent stealing /

そしてお金を盗む試みを記録するために / レジから
and to record attempts to steal money / from the

cash register. //

現在、それらのカメラが違う目的で使われている
Now those same cameras are serving another

/ それらは見ている / どのように買い物をするか // それら
purpose: / they are watching / how we shop. // They

は記録する / 何人の人が店に入るか / 毎時間、開店し
record / how many people enter a store / each hour it

ている間 // マネージャーはこのデータを使うことができる / スタッフのスケジュ
is open. // Managers can use this data / to make staff

ールを組むために // 大勢の人々が来るとき / マネージャーは確信が
schedules. // When crowds come, / the managers

持てる / 店員が足りることを /
can be sure / that there will be enough salespeople /

客に対応するための // いくつかの店のカメラは / 判別すること
to serve them. // Cameras in some shops / are able to

06 スラッシュ訳

determine / customers' ethnicity. // Noticing / that groups of tourists from one foreign country / came in the shop at the same time every day, / the manager posted sales staff / who could speak their language. // Cameras also observe / what products we look at / and how we move through the store. // Managers use this data / to decide / where to place goods on shelves / and how to attract the customer's attention. // Some stores have installed widescreen monitors / to show / floor plans and advertisements for special sale items. // Behind each monitor is a camera / which notes eye movement. / The camera tries to determine / the viewer's gender and age group. // On the basis of this data, / the screen then changes / to show advertisements for products / that the person might like. //

Recently some stores track signals / from cell phones. // They can find out / how many people / walking by their store / actually come in. // They can count / how many minutes a person stays in the store, too. // Although the store managers do not know / who owns the phone, / they do know / how frequently the phone / —and its owner— / enters the store. // In other words, / they can recognize repeat customers. // Shop managers find this information very helpful / for their business. //

06 和訳 & 解答

あなたを監視している

　私達はどこに行っても監視されている。防犯カメラが、会議室、レストランや地下鉄の駅で、私達を録画している。これらのカメラは、人々を守って犯罪を防止するために設置されている。商店においては、カメラは盗難を防いだり、レジからお金を盗もうと企てるのを録画したりするために使われている。

　現在、同様のカメラが、別の目的でも使われている。私達がどのように買い物をするかを観察しているのだ。カメラは営業中の1時間ごとに何人が入店するかを記録する。店のマネージャーはそれをもとにしてスタッフのシフトを組めるので、混み合う時間帯に、対応するのに十分な人数の販売員を揃えておくことが確実にできる。顧客の人種を識別できるカメラを設置している店もある。ある国からの観光客グループが毎日同じ時間に来店することに気づいたマネージャーは、彼らの言語を話せる販売員を配置した。

　カメラは私達がどんな商品を見て、どのように店内を動きまわるかも観察している。マネージャーはこのデータから、棚のどこに商品を配置し、どのように顧客の興味をひくかを決定する。フロアの見取り図と特別セール商品の広告を流す大画面モニターを設置している店もある。各モニターの裏にはカメラがあって、見る人の目の動きを観察し、性別や年齢層も判別する。このデータをもとに、画面がその人の好みに合うと推測される商品の広告に切り替わるのだ。

　最近は、携帯電話の信号を追跡している店もある。店の前を通りかかる人のうちの何人が実際に店に入ってくるかがわかるのだ。一人のお客が何分間店内にとどまるかも計算できる。店のマネージャーにはその携帯電話の持ち主が誰なのかはわからないが、その携帯電話が―そしてその所有者が―どのくらい頻繁に入店するかはわかる。言い換えると、常連客がわかるのだ。店のマネージャーは、この情報は商売のうえで非常に有益であると感じている。

True or False　解答 & 和訳

1. T　防犯カメラは、犯罪を防ぐために使われている。
2. F　カメラのデータは、経営者が仕事をする手助けをしていない。
3. NS　ショーウィンドーにはカメラが備え付けられている。
4. T　大画面モニターは、ときどき特売品を映し出している。
5. NS　携帯電話からの信号を追跡することは法に反する。
6. F　店の経営者は、携帯電話の持ち主の名前を知っている。

Unit 07

Revolution in Color
— 売れる色、速い色、隠せる色 —

revolution	名 革命	manufacturer	名 メーカー
study	動 研究する	various	形 多様な
focus on ~	~に焦点を絞る	attractive	形 魅力的な
everyday life	日々の生活	among ~ were	~の中に含まれていた
comfortable	形 快適な	illusion	名 錯覚
convenient	形 便利な	streamlined	形 流線型の
colorist	名 色彩の専門家	share	名 取り分
specialist	名 専門家	human psychology	人間の心理
shape	動 形成する	make efforts	努力する
consumer	名 消費者	predict	動 予測する
cute	形 かわいい	in the years to come	近い将来に

Revolution in Color

The revolution in the use of colors has not been carefully studied for several reasons. First, the color revolution is something that has happened in the business world. Second, people who study design often focus on the actual products that make everyday life more comfortable and convenient. Or they focus on modern ideas of what is beautiful or useful. These researchers have not paid much attention to the revolution in the use of color itself.

Professional colorists have mostly worked behind closed doors with other specialists. Few people see what they do. But what they have done has shaped our environment in many ways. Consumer products from children's toys to laptop computers to cute cars have come directly from their ideas.

They have helped schools, car manufacturers, and telephone engineers master the various effects of color. They have worked to make houses feel warm and comfortable. They have studied how to make office space and classrooms safe and ideal for reading and working. They have developed attractive clothing that

Round 1	Round 2	Round 3	Round 4	Round 5	Round 6
WPM 語	WPM 語	WPM 語	WPM 語	WPM 語	WPM 語
月 日	月 日	月 日	月 日	月 日	月 日

brings customers into department stores.

　　Among the first colorists were people who used their artistic talents during World War I. They used color and illusion to develop camouflage to hide weapons and soldiers. After the war, some of these colorists worked in the auto industry. They used color to make cars look slimmer, faster, and more streamlined. They also selected colors that buyers would want to buy.

　　Each industry has its own share of professional colorists who study market surveys and sales reports. They look at data to see which colors are popular on packages and on the products themselves. They study human psychology to learn what combinations and patterns of color attract the eye and make a person want to buy a product. And they make efforts to predict which colors will become popular in the years to come.

312 words

07 True or False?

次の1～6の文を読み、本文の内容に合っていたらT、合わなかったらF、述べられていなかったらNS（Not stated）を選んでください。

---

1 Major changes in the use of color are not well researched.

- T ☐
- F ☐
- NS ☐

2 Colorists usually work in places where they are carefully observed.

- T ☐
- F ☐
- NS ☐

3 Professional colorists have worked with cosmetic manufacturers.

- T ☐
- F ☐
- NS ☐

4 Professional colorists have helped to make attractive clothes.

- T ☐
- F ☐
- NS ☐

5 Colors can make cars look like they are faster.

- T ☐
- F ☐
- NS ☐

6 Colorists help companies select attractive colors for products.

- T ☐
- F ☐
- NS ☐

スラッシュ訳

file-14

色彩革命
Revolution in Color

The revolution in the use of colors / has not been carefully studied / for several reasons. // First, / the color revolution is something / that has happened in the business world. // Second, / people who study design / often focus on the actual products / that make everyday life more comfortable and convenient. // Or they focus on modern ideas / of what is beautiful or useful. // These researchers have not paid much attention / to the revolution in the use of color itself. // Professional colorists have mostly worked / behind closed doors / with other specialists. // Few people see / what they do. // But what they have done / has shaped our environment / in many ways. // Consumer products / from children's toys / to laptop computers

07 スラッシュ訳

to cute cars / have come directly from their ideas. //
They have helped / schools, car manufacturers, and telephone engineers / master the various effects of color. // They have worked / to make houses feel warm and comfortable. // They have studied / how to make office space and classrooms safe / and ideal for reading and working. // They have developed attractive clothing / that brings customers into department stores. //
Among the first colorists were people / who used their artistic talents / during World War I. // They used color and illusion / to develop camouflage / to hide weapons and soldiers. // After the war, / some of these colorists worked in the auto industry. // They used color / to make cars look / slimmer, faster, and more streamlined. // They also selected colors / that buyers would want to buy. //

　　　　それぞれの業界は一定数を擁している　　　　プロの色彩専門家
　　Each industry has its own share / of professional
　　　　　　　　市場調査や売上報告書を詳しく調べる
　　colorists / who study market surveys and sales
　　　　　　　　彼らはデータを見る　　　　見るため　どの色がパッケージ
　　reports. ∥ They look at data / to see / which colors
　　で人気があるか　　　　　　　　　　　　そして商品自体
　　are popular on packages / and on the products
　　　　　　　　　　彼らは人間の心理を研究する
　　themselves. ∥ They study human psychology / to
　　知るため　どんな色の組み合わせやパターンが目を引きつけるか
　　learn / what combinations and patterns of color
　　　　　　　　　　　　そして人にその商品を買いたくさせるか
　　attract the eye / and make a person want to buy a
　　　　　　　　そして彼らは努力する　　　　　予測するため
　　product. ∥ And they make efforts / to predict / which
　　どの色が近い将来人気が出るか
　　colors will become popular in the years to come. ∥

07 和訳 & 解答

色彩革命

　色の使い方における革命が入念に研究されていないのには、いくつかの理由がある。まず、色彩革命は、ビジネス界で起こったことだからだ。次に、デザインの研究者たちは、日常生活をより快適で便利にする製品それ自体や、美とはなにかまたは役に立つとはどういうことかという現代的なアイデアに注目しがちである。これらの研究者たちは、色の使い方の革命自体には注意を払わなかった。

　プロの色彩専門家たちは、他の専門家たちと共にもっぱら裏方として働いてきた。その仕事内容を知る人はほとんどいない。しかし彼らの仕事は、色々な面で我々の環境を形作ってきた。子供のおもちゃやノートパソコンからかわいい車にいたるまでの消費者製品は、彼らのアイデアから生まれてきた。

　彼らは、学校、自動車メーカーや電話技師が色の様々な効果を習得するのを助けた。また、家を暖かくて快適に感じさせることに取り組んできた。オフィス空間や教室を安全で読書や仕事に適した場にする方法を研究した。デパートに顧客を呼び寄せる魅力的な衣類を開発した。

　最初の色彩専門家たちの中には、第一次世界大戦中に彼らの芸術的才能を用いた人々もいた。彼らは色と錯覚を利用して、武器と兵士を隠すためのカモフラージュを開発した。戦争の後、一部の色彩専門家は自動車産業で働いた。色を用いて、車がよりスリムで速く、流線形に見えるようにした。また、買い手が買いたがるような色も選んだ。

　それぞれの産業には、市場調査と販売報告書を詳しく調べるプロの色彩専門家がいる。彼らはパッケージと製品自体にどの色が人気なのかを探るため、データを見る。彼らは色のどの組合せとパターンが人目を引いて購買意欲を促すかを知るため、人間の心理を研究する。そして、近い将来どの色が流行るかを予測すべく努力する。

True or False　解答 & 和訳

1. T　色の使い方の大きな変化については、よく研究されていない。
2. F　色彩専門家はふつう、彼らが注意深く観察される場所で仕事をしている。
3. NS　プロの色彩専門家は化粧品製造業者と仕事をしてきた。
4. T　プロの色彩専門家は魅力的な服をつくるのを助けた。
5. T　色によって、車がより速いかのように見せることができる。
6. T　色彩専門家は、企業が商品に魅力的な色を選ぶことを助ける。

Unit 08

Under the Sea
— シーグライダーで海を調べよ! —

crew	名 乗組員	pollution	名 汚染
sophisticated	形 精巧な	recharge	動 再充電する
instrument	名 機器	if necessary	必要であれば
surface	名 表面	considering	前 ～を考慮して
companion	名 仲間	explore	動 探索する
unmanned	形 無人の	intelligence	名 機密情報
vessel	名 船舶	spot	動 見つける
Atlantic Ocean	大西洋	identify	動 認識する
iceberg	名 氷山	at present	現在では
school of fish	魚の群れ	fishing net	漁網

08 速読

Under the Sea

Submarines carrying large crews and sophisticated instruments travel around the world under the surface of the sea. Now they have small silent companions called "sea gliders." Hundreds of these unmanned vessels are currently at work.

The typical sea glider looks like a rocket. Its small wings guide it through the water. It travels very slowly at less than one kilometer per hour. It uses an extremely small amount of power. As a result, it can stay out in the ocean for months at a time. In 2009 a glider used a single battery charge to travel across the Atlantic Ocean. It took seven months to go across.

Sea gliders are already helping scientists do many things that were not possible before. These vessels can watch underwater volcanoes. They can measure the size of an iceberg. They can follow a school of fish. They can track the effects of pollution in water at various depths. Scientists are beginning to use them to create maps of the ocean floor.

Gliders are already able to carry out missions that last several months. But now a researcher in Japan is at work on a solar-powered glider called SORA. This vessel rises to the surface for a few days to recharge, then continues its work. As a result, it can stay at sea for years if necessary.

Currently, sea gliders cost about $150,000 to produce, but that cost is very small considering what they can do. Businesses can use them to survey the ocean floor to explore for oil and gas. Governments can use them to gather intelligence. Without being spotted, a glider can identify ships on the surface or manned submarines that pass near it.

At present, the only enemies of the sea gliders are fishing nets and sharks. But if the number of these gliders increases, there may be a traffic jam at rush hour.

315 words

08 True or False?

次の1～6の文を読み、本文の内容に合っていたらT、合わなかったらF、述べられていなかったらNS（Not stated）を選んでください。

1	Sea gliders carry small crews with sophisticated instruments.	T ☐ F ☐ NS ☐
2	These small gliders can operate for months with just one battery charge.	T ☐ F ☐ NS ☐
3	Studying volcanoes is the most valuable job they can do.	T ☐ F ☐ NS ☐
4	Sea gliders help scientists study the ocean floor.	T ☐ F ☐ NS ☐
5	Governments use sea gliders to get information about ships and submarines.	T ☐ F ☐ NS ☐
6	Sea gliders sometimes break fishing nets.	T ☐ F ☐ NS ☐

スラッシュ訳

Under the Sea
海の中で

大人数の乗組員と精巧な機器を積んでいる潜水艦が
Submarines carrying large crews and sophisticated instruments / *世界中を回る* travel around the world / *海の表面の下で* under the surface of the sea. // *今、彼らには音を出さない小さな仲間がいる* Now they have small silent companions / *「シーグライダー」と呼ばれている* called "sea gliders." // *何百ものこれらの* Hundreds of *無人の船舶が現在、使われている* these unmanned vessels are currently at work. //

典型的なシーグライダーはロケットのように見える The typical sea glider looks like a rocket. // *その小さい翼がそれを導く* Its small wings guide it / *水の中を通って* through the water. // *それはとてもゆっくり進む* It travels very slowly / *時速1キロ未満で* at less than one kilometer per hour. // *それは極めて少ない量の電力を使う* It uses an extremely small amount of power. // *その結果* As a result, / *それは外洋に留まることができる* it can stay out in the ocean / *1回に何カ月も* for months at a time. // *2009年に* In 2009 / *あるグライダーは1回のみ充電を使った* a glider used a single battery charge / *大西洋を横断するのに* to travel across the Atlantic Ocean. // *それは7カ月かかった* It took seven months / *渡るのに* to go across. //

シーグライダーはもうすでに科学者を助けている
Sea gliders are already helping scientists / do

08 スラッシュ訳

many things / that were not possible before. // These
vessels can watch underwater volcanoes. // They can
measure the size of an iceberg. // They can follow a
school of fish. // They can track the effects / of pollution
in water / at various depths. // Scientists are beginning
to use them / to create maps of the ocean floor. //
Gliders are already able to carry out missions / that
last several months. // But now / a researcher in Japan
is / at work on / a solar-powered glider called SORA. //
This vessel rises to the surface / for a few days / to
recharge, / then continues its work. // As a result, / it
can stay at sea for years / if necessary. //
Currently, / sea gliders cost about $150,000 / to
produce, / but that cost is very small / considering what
they can do. // Businesses can use them / to survey the
ocean floor / to explore for oil and gas. // Governments

can use them / to gather intelligence. // Without being spotted, / a glider can identify ships / on the surface / or manned submarines / that pass near it. //

At present, / the only enemies of the sea gliders are / fishing nets and sharks. // But if the number of these gliders increases, / there may be a traffic jam at rush hour. //

08 和訳＆解答

海の中で

　多数の乗組員と精巧な機器を積んだ潜水艦が、世界中で海面下を潜航している。今それらに、「シーグライダー」と呼ばれる小型の音を立てない仲間が加わった。現在これらの無人船は数百艇も稼働している。

　一般的なシーグライダーの外観はロケットに似ている。その小さな翼で水中を進み、毎時1キロメートル未満で非常にゆっくり移動する。電力消費量はきわめて少ない。結果として、それは一度に何カ月も海中に留まることができる。2009年には、一艇のシーグライダーが、一回のバッテリー充電のみで大西洋を横断した。横断には7カ月かかった。

　シーグライダーのおかげですでに科学者たちは、以前には不可能だった多くのことができるようになっている。シーグライダーは、海底火山を観察することができる。氷山の大きさを測ることができる。魚の群れを追うことができる。さまざまな深度で水中の汚染の影響を監視することができる。科学者たちは、シーグライダーを利用して海底の地図を作成することまでも始めている。

　シーグライダーはすでに、数カ月も継続する任務を遂行することが可能になっている。しかし、日本の研究者は現在、SORAと呼ばれる太陽光発電を使ったグライダーを開発中で、この船は再充電のために2、3日間海面に出れば、その後は作業を続けられる。結果として、必要ならば何年も海に留まることができる。

　現在、シーグライダーを製造するのにおよそ15万ドル費用がかかるが、それがなし得ることを考えればその費用は非常に小さい。シーグライダーを使えば、企業は石油とガスの探索のために海底調査ができるし、政府は機密情報を収集できる。グライダーは、見つかることなく海面にいる船や近くを通り過ぎる有人潜水艦を特定できる。

　現時点では、シーグライダーの唯一の敵は、魚網とサメだけだ。しかし、もしグライダーの数が増加すれば、ラッシュ時には交通渋滞がおきるかもしれない。

True or False　解答＆和訳

1. F　シーグライダーは洗練された道具と一緒に、小さな乗組員も乗せる。
2. T　それらの小さなグライダーは、たった1回の充電で何カ月も操縦できる。
3. NS　火山を研究することは、彼らができる最も価値ある仕事だ。
4. T　シーグライダーは科学者が海底の調査をするのを助ける。
5. T　政府は、シーグライダーを船舶や潜水艦の情報を得るために使う。
6. NS　シーグライダーは、ときどき、漁網を破る。

Unit 09

The Right Sound
― うるさくもなく、静かすぎもせず ―

designer	名 設計者	stressful	形 ストレスの多い
increasingly	副 ますます	concentration	名 集中
broad	形 広い	fatigue	名 疲労
affect	動 影響を与える	complete	形 完全な
air pollution	大気汚染	pedestrian	名 歩行者
noise pollution	騒音公害	blind	形 目の不自由な
expensive	形 高価な	dangerous	形 危険な
consume	動 消費する	vehicle	名 乗り物
operate	動 運転する	desirable	形 好ましい
decrease	動 減る	necessary	形 必要な

09 速読

The Right Sound

Designers are increasingly paying attention to making products that make less noise. Steve Jobs, for example, did not want to use a fan to cool his first computer. He thought a fan would make too much noise. Since then, there has been a broad movement to make products that are quieter.

The reason for doing this is clear: noise is a problem that affects us all. In 2011 the World Health Organization published a report on health and the environment. The main environmental cause of bad health is air pollution. The second cause is noise pollution. Making a quieter environment is good for people and for businesses, too. Quieter cars, printers, washing machines, and airplanes may be more expensive, but these products consume less energy. That makes them cheaper to operate in the long run.

Quieter airplanes, as one example, are better for everyone. People who live near airports are happier when noise decreases. People who fly on quieter planes find traveling less stressful, too. In the workplace, machinery and air conditioning that is quieter may be a bit more expensive, but it increases concentration and reduces fatigue.

In general, noise is bad, but complete silence is not good either. For pedestrians and people who are blind, quiet electric cars and electric bicycles can be dangerous. It is important for such vehicles to make at least some sound for safety reasons. To let the user know that he or she has taken a photo, an artificial sound is added to digital cameras.

There are other cases where sound is desirable even though it is not necessary. Car manufacturers work hard so that the closing of the car door sounds just right. They want to produce a sound that produces a feeling of high quality.

For designers, the goal is not silence, but getting the sound right. And most of the time, "right" means quieter and making less noise.

321 words

09 True or False?

次の1〜6の文を読み、本文の内容に合っていたらT、合わなかったらF、述べられていなかったらNS（Not stated）を選んでください。

---

1. Fans used to cool computers do not make noise.

   T ☐
   F ☐
   NS ☐

2. Noise is one of the major environmental causes of bad health.

   T ☐
   F ☐
   NS ☐

3. Airplanes that are quieter use less energy.

   T ☐
   F ☐
   NS ☐

4. Quieter workplaces help increase concentration.

   T ☐
   F ☐
   NS ☐

5. Quiet cars and bicycles are safer.

   T ☐
   F ☐
   NS ☐

6. The right sound can make a car seem like it is high quality.

   T ☐
   F ☐
   NS ☐

スラッシュ訳

The Right Sound
適切な音

Designers are increasingly paying attention / to making products / that make less noise. // Steve Jobs, / for example, / did not want to use a fan / to cool his first computer. // He thought / a fan would make too much noise. // Since then, / there has been a broad movement / to make products / that are quieter. //

The reason for doing this is clear: / noise is a problem / that affects us all. // In 2011 / the World Health Organization published a report / on health and the environment. // The main environmental cause of bad health / is air pollution. // The second cause is noise pollution. // Making a quieter environment / is good for people and for businesses,

09 スラッシュ訳

too. // Quieter cars, printers, washing machines, and airplanes / may be more expensive, / but these products consume less energy. // That makes them cheaper to operate / in the long run. //

Quieter airplanes, / as one example, / are better for everyone. // People who live near airports / are happier / when noise decreases. // People who fly on quieter planes / find traveling less stressful, too. // In the workplace, / machinery and air conditioning / that is quieter / may be a bit more expensive, / but it increases concentration and reduces fatigue. //

In general, noise is bad, / but complete silence is not good either. // For pedestrians and people who are blind, / quiet electric cars and electric bicycles can be dangerous. // It is important / for such vehicles / to make at least some sound for safety reasons. // To let

<ruby>the user know<rt>利用者に知らせるため</rt></ruby> / <ruby>that he or she has taken a photo,<rt>その人が写真を撮ったことを</rt></ruby> / <ruby>an artificial sound is added<rt>人工的な音が加えられている</rt></ruby> / <ruby>to digital cameras.<rt>デジタルカメラに</rt></ruby> //
<ruby>There are other cases<rt>他の場合がある</rt></ruby> / <ruby>where sound is desirable<rt>音が好ましい</rt></ruby> / <ruby>even though it is not necessary.<rt>それが必要ないにも関わらず</rt></ruby> // <ruby>Car manufacturers work hard<rt>自動車メーカーは努力する</rt></ruby> / <ruby>so that the closing of the car door sounds just right.<rt>車のドアを閉める音がちょうど良いものになるように</rt></ruby> // <ruby>They want to produce a sound<rt>彼らは音を作りたい</rt></ruby> / that <ruby>produces a feeling of high quality.<rt>高級感を出すもの</rt></ruby> //

<ruby>For designers,<rt>設計者にとって</rt></ruby> / <ruby>the goal is not silence,<rt>目標は無音ではない</rt></ruby> / <ruby>but getting the sound right.<rt>むしろ適切な音だ</rt></ruby> // <ruby>And most of the time,<rt>そしてほとんどの場合</rt></ruby> / <ruby>"right" means quieter and making less noise.<rt>「適切」はより静かで騒がしくないことを意味する</rt></ruby> //

09 和訳 & 解答

適切な音

　設計技術者たちは、音を出さない製品を作ろうとますます努力するようになっている。たとえばスティーブ・ジョブズは、彼の最初のコンピュータの冷却にファンを使用するのを嫌った。ファンはうるさ過ぎると思ったのだ。以来、より静かな製品を作ろうという動きが広く見られる。

　静かな製品をつくろうとする理由は明白だ。騒音は誰にも影響を及ぼす問題だからだ。2011年に世界保健機構は、健康と環境についての報告書を発表した。健康を害する一番の環境的原因は大気汚染で、2番目が騒音公害である。騒音の少ない環境を作ることは、人にも企業にも良いことだ。騒音の少ない車、プリンター、洗濯機や飛行機は高価かもしれない。しかし消費するエネルギーが少ないので、長期的に見れば運転費は比較的安い。

　例をあげれば、騒音の少ない飛行機は誰にとっても好ましい。騒音が減れば、空港の近隣住民にとっては嬉しいことだ。騒音の少ない飛行機の乗客もストレスが少ないと感じるだろう。職場では、騒音の少ない機械や空調は若干高価かもしれないが、集中力を高めて疲労を軽減してくれる。

　一般的に騒音は好ましくないが、完全な無音も良くはない。歩行者や視覚障害者にとって、静かな電気自動車や電動自転車は危険な場合がある。そういった乗り物は、安全上の理由のために最低限の音を出すことが必要なのだ。デジタルカメラには、写真が撮れたことを使用者がわかるように人工の音が加えられている。

　たとえ必要ではなくとも、音が出るほうが望ましい場合は他にもある。自動車メーカーは、車のドアを閉める際に適切な音がするよう、懸命に取り組んでいる。高品質な感じの音を作り出したいのだ。

　設計技術者が目指すゴールは無音でなく、適切な音だ。そしてほとんどの場合、適切とは、より静かでより騒音が少ないことを意味する。

True or False　解答 & 和訳

1. F　コンピュータを冷やすためのファンは音を立てない。
2. T　騒音は環境汚染の2番目の悪因だ。
3. T　より静かな飛行機は、エネルギーの消費量が少ない。
4. T　より静かな職場は、集中力を上げるのに役立つ。
5. F　静かな車や自転車は、より安全だ。
6. T　適切な音は、車を高性能であるように見せることができる。

Unit 10

Musical Medicine
― 治療を助ける音楽セラピスト ―

treat	動 治療する	in one way or another	何らかの形で
patient	名 患者	anxious	形 不安な
musical instrument	楽器	distract	動 気を散らす
sing along	合わせて歌う	blood pressure	血圧
all the way	最後まで	biofeedback	バイオフィードバック
frightening	形 怖い		（生体自己制御法：生理活動を機器により音楽などの知覚可能な情報に変換するセルフコントロール技法）
catch on	広まる		
psychologist	名 心理学者	consciously	副 意識的に
anxiety	名 不安	slow down	速度を落とす
relate to ~	~感じることができる	lower	動 低くする

10 速読

Musical Medicine

Boston Children's Hospital has a staff member with an unusual job. He is not a doctor but he helps treat young patients at the hospital. He does this with his voice, a guitar, and other musical instruments. He is what is called a music therapist.

For example, he helped a 4-year-old patient at the hospital who was worried about having an X-ray taken. The music therapist came to her room and they began singing a song together with his guitar. The song continued as they got on the elevator. The girl, the therapist, the girl's parents, and the nurse were all singing along. The X-ray was taken and they sang all the way back to the little girl's room. For the young patient, the X-ray was no longer a frightening experience.

The idea of using music to help young patients is catching on. Psychologists say that music has the ability to reduce anxiety. It works because everyone relates to music in one way or another. And it works in different ways. If the patient is anxious about something, music with a fast tempo helps distract them.

Round 1	Round 2	Round 3	Round 4	Round 5	Round 6
WPM 語	WPM 語	WPM 語	WPM 語	WPM 語	WPM 語
月 日	月 日	月 日	月 日	月 日	月 日

If the patient needs to relax, then music with a slower tempo helps them do that, too.

Some music therapists work with adults, too. Adult patients write words and the therapist and the patient try to put music to the words. As they create a song together, they talk about the meaning of the words. This is one way for the therapist to learn what the patient is worried about.

Music therapists can also help adult patients learn how to relax. The speed and tone of the song that a patient and therapist sing or play can change the patient's heart rate. It can also help lower blood pressure. By using biofeedback, the patient can learn to consciously slow down his heart rate and lower his blood pressure. It's done by changing the music—and enjoying it.

326 words

10 True or False?

次の 1 〜 6 の文を読み、本文の内容に合っていたら T、合わなかったら F、述べられていなかったら NS (Not stated) を選んでください。

1	The musical therapist is a doctor.	T ☐ F ☐ NS ☐
2	The musical therapist performs at a charity event.	T ☐ F ☐ NS ☐
3	Music can be used to make an X-ray less frightening.	T ☐ F ☐ NS ☐
4	Everyone relates to music in the same way.	T ☐ F ☐ NS ☐
5	Musical therapy is used with adults and children.	T ☐ F ☐ NS ☐
6	Music cannot be used to change blood pressure.	T ☐ F ☐ NS ☐

スラッシュ訳

音楽療法
Musical Medicine

Boston Children's Hospital / has a staff member with an unusual job. // He is not a doctor / but he helps / treat young patients / at the hospital. // He does this / with his voice, a guitar, and other musical instruments. // He is what is called a music therapist. //

For example, / he helped / a 4-year-old patient / at the hospital / who was worried about having an X-ray taken. // The music therapist came / to her room / and they began singing a song together / with his guitar. // The song continued / as they got on the elevator. // The girl, the therapist, the girl's parents, and the nurse / were all singing along. // The X-ray was taken / and they sang / all the way / back to the

10 スラッシュ訳

little girl's room. // For the young patient, / the X-ray
was no longer a frightening experience. //
　The idea of using music / to help young patients / is
catching on. // Psychologists say / that music has the
ability / to reduce anxiety. // It works / because /
everyone relates to music / in one way or another. //
And it works / in different ways. // If the patient is
anxious about something, / music with a fast tempo
helps / distract them. // If the patient needs to relax, /
then music with a slower tempo helps them /
do that, too. //
　Some music therapists work with adults, too. // Adult
patients write words / and the therapist and the patient
try to put music to the words. // As they create a song
together, / they talk about the meaning of the words. //
This is one way for the therapist / to learn / what the

<ruby>patient is worried about.<rt>しているかを</rt></ruby> //

<ruby>Music therapists can also help<rt>また、音楽療法士は助けることができる</rt></ruby> / <ruby>adult patients<rt>成人患者を</rt></ruby> / <ruby>learn how to relax.<rt>どうやってリラックスできるか学ぶ</rt></ruby> // <ruby>The speed and tone of the song<rt>歌のスピードと曲調が</rt></ruby> / <ruby>that a patient and therapist sing or play<rt>患者と療法士が歌ったり演奏したりする</rt></ruby> / <ruby>can change the patient's heart rate.<rt>患者の心拍数を変えることができる</rt></ruby> // <ruby>It can also help lower blood pressure.<rt>それは血圧を下げることもできる</rt></ruby> // <ruby>By using biofeedback,<rt>バイオフィードバックを使うことで</rt></ruby> / the <ruby>patient can learn<rt>患者は学ぶことができる</rt></ruby> / <ruby>to consciously slow down his heart rate<rt>意識的に心拍数を落とし</rt></ruby> / <ruby>and lower his blood pressure.<rt>そして血圧を下げる</rt></ruby> // <ruby>It's done<rt>それはできる</rt></ruby> / by <ruby>changing the music<rt>音楽をかえることで</rt></ruby> / <ruby>—and enjoying it.<rt>そしてそれを楽しむことで</rt></ruby> //

10 和訳 & 解答

音楽療法

　ボストン小児病院には、変わった仕事をする職員がいる。彼は医師ではないが、病院で幼い患者の治療を助けている。歌とギターやその他の楽器で治療を手助けする、いわゆる音楽療法士だ。

　たとえば彼は、病院でレントゲン検査を怖がる4歳の患者の手助けをした。この音楽療法士が彼女の部屋に来ると、二人は彼のギターに合わせて一緒に歌を歌い始めた。二人はエレベーターに乗っても歌い続けた。女の子、セラピスト、女の子の両親と看護師が皆で一緒に歌った。レントゲン撮影がすんで女の子の病室に戻るまでも、皆はずっと歌い続けた。この幼い患者にとって、レントゲンはもはや怖い体験ではなくなっていた。

　幼い患者を助けるために音楽を使うというアイデアは広まりつつある。心理学者によれば、音楽には不安をやわらげる力があるという。誰でも音楽には何かしら共感を覚えるので、効果があるのだ。その効き方も様々だ。患者に何か心配ごとがあれば、速いテンポの音楽が気を紛らわせてくれる。リラックスする必要のある患者には、遅めのテンポの音楽が役立つ。

　成人も対象とする音楽療法士がいる。成人患者が歌詞を書いて、療法士と患者とで曲をつけてみる。一緒に歌を作りながら、歌詞の意味について語り合う。これは療法士が患者の悩みを知る方法のひとつだ。

　音楽療法士は、成人患者がリラックスする方法を学ぶ手助けもできる。患者と療法士が歌ったり演奏したりする歌の速さと曲調が、心拍数を変えたり、血圧を下げたりする効果がある。バイオフィードバックを用いることで、患者は意識的に心拍数を落とし、血圧を下げることができるようになる。音楽を変えて、それを楽しむことで、それが可能となる。

True or False　解答 & 和訳

1. F　音楽療法士は医師だ。
2. NS　音楽療法士は、チャリティイベントで演奏する。
3. T　音楽は、レントゲンに対する恐れを軽減するのに使うことができる。
4. F　誰もが同じ方法で音楽と関わっている。
5. T　音楽療法は大人にも子どもにも使われる。
6. F　音楽を使って血圧を変えることはできない。

Unit 11

Coming Up with Ideas
— 創造力と集中とリラックス —

come up with ~	(考えなどが)浮かぶ	transition	名 移行
creativity	名 創造力	fall asleep	眠りに落ちる
born with ~	~を持って生まれる	psychologist	名 心理学者
have an advantage	優位に立つ	improve	動 高める
curious	形 好奇心の強い	regularly	副 定期的に
interested	形 興味を持っている	completely	副 完全に
solve	動 解く	physical	形 肉体的な
focus on ~	~に集中する	connection	名 つながり
creative	形 創造性に富む	occur to ~	~が気付く
wander	動 さまよう	solution	名 解決策

Coming Up with Ideas

Some people come up with new ideas very easily. Others try hard, but can't come up with any ideas at all. Is creativity something we are born with? Or is it something that we can all develop?

Personality can make a difference. A person who is open to new experiences may have an advantage. He or she may be more curious and more interested in new ways of doing things. But personality isn't the only key to creativity.

Many people think that the best way to solve a problem is to focus on it. However, sometimes the best way to be creative is to walk away from a problem. Just let your mind wander while you do something else. In fact, a lot of great ideas come at times of transition. These include when you are waking up in the morning, falling asleep at night, or taking a shower. By not focusing attention on a problem, you may open your mind to new ways of solving it.

Psychologists studying creativity have also found that the color green may help people come up with creative ideas. One group of psychologists gave students a creativity test. The only difference was that there were different colors on the test cover page. The test cover pages were black, white, red, gray and green. Students with green test cover pages had more creative ideas than those with other colors.

Another way to improve creativity is to regularly make time for letting your mind wander. Go for a walk, look out a window, or do something completely physical. In other words, let your brain have a rest. This allows your brain to make connections that didn't occur to you when you were focusing. If you don't take a break, then your brain will not be creative. So don't be afraid to put a problem to one side for a few minutes. It may be the best way to find a good solution to the problem.

333 words

11 True or False?

次の1〜6の文を読み、本文の内容に合っていたらT、合わなかったらF、述べられていなかったらNS (Not stated) を選んでください。

1	If people don't try hard, they cannot come up with new ideas.	T ☐ F ☐ NS ☐
2	Creativity depends completely on personality.	T ☐ F ☐ NS ☐
3	Many good ideas come during times when you are doing something else.	T ☐ F ☐ NS ☐
4	Coming up with creative ideas may be related to colors in some way.	T ☐ F ☐ NS ☐
5	Letting the mind wander regularly is bad for creativity.	T ☐ F ☐ NS ☐
6	Studying psychology improves your creativity.	T ☐ F ☐ NS ☐

スラッシュ訳

file-22

Coming Up with Ideas
アイデアが浮かぶ

Some people come up with new ideas / very easily. //
新しいアイデアが浮かぶ人がいる / とても簡単に

Others try hard, / but can't come up with any ideas at
他の人は懸命にやろうとする / しかし全くアイデアが浮かんでこない

all. // Is creativity something / we are born with? // Or
創造性は何か / 我々が持って生まれる

is it something / that we can all develop? //
またはそれは何か / 我々が発展させることができる

Personality can make a difference. // A person /
性格は違いを生む / ある人は

who is open to new experiences / may have an
新しい経験を受け入れる人 / 優位に立つかも

advantage. // He or she may be more curious / and
しれない / その人は好奇心が強いかもしれない / そして

more interested / in new ways / of doing things. //
より興味がある / 新しいやり方に / 物事を行う

But personality isn't the only key / to creativity. //
しかし性格だけが鍵ではない / 創造力の

Many people think / that the best way / to solve a
多くの人は考える / 最良の方法は / 問題を解決す

problem / is to focus on it. // However, / sometimes /
るため / それに集中することだ / しかし / 時々

the best way / to be creative / is to walk away / from
最良の方法は / 創造的になるための / 遠ざかること /

a problem. // Just let your mind wander / while you
問題から / ただあなたの心をさまよわせなさい / あなたが何か

do something else. // In fact, / a lot of great ideas /
別のことをする間 / 実は / たくさんの素晴らしいアイデア

11 スラッシュ訳

come at times of transition. // These include / when you are waking up in the morning, / falling asleep at night, / or taking a shower. // By not focusing attention on a problem, / you may open your mind / to new ways of solving it. //

Psychologists studying creativity have also found / that the color green may help people / come up with creative ideas. // One group of psychologists gave students / a creativity test. // The only difference was / that there were different colors / on the test cover page. // The test cover pages were black, white, red, gray and green. // Students with green test cover pages / had more creative ideas / than those with other colors. //

Another way to improve creativity is / to regularly make time / for letting your mind wander. // Go for a walk, / look out a window, / or do something completely physical. // In other words, / let your brain have a rest. // This allows your brain / to make connections / that didn't occur to you / when you were focusing. // If you don't take a break, / then your brain will not be creative. // So don't be afraid / to put a problem to one side / for a few minutes. // It may be the best way / to find a good solution / to the problem. //

11　和訳 & 解答

アイデアを出す方法

　簡単に新しいアイデアを出せる人もいれば、懸命に頑張っても全く何も浮かばない人もいる。創造力とは生まれつきの能力なのだろうか。それとも、誰でも創造力を発達させることができるものなのだろうか。

　その人の性格によっても違いが出る。新しいことを受け入れられるタイプは有利かもしれない。そういう人はより好奇心が旺盛で、新しいやり方に興味を持つかもしれない。だが創造力の鍵を握るのは性格だけではない。

　多くの人々は、問題を解決する最良の方法はそれに集中することだと考えている。だが時には、問題を置いておくことが創造力を引き出す最良の方法になる場合もある。何か他のことをして、心をさまよわせてみる。実は、移行の時間に素晴らしいアイデアが浮かぶことは多い。朝目が覚める時や、夜に眠りにつく時、シャワーを浴びている時などもそうだ。問題に意識を集中しないことで、新たな解決方法に心が開かれるのかもしれない。

　創造力を研究する心理学者たちは、緑色が創造的なアイデアを出す助けになるかもしれないと見ている。心理学者のグループが、複数の学生を相手に創造力テストを行ったのだが、テスト冊子の表紙の色だけが異なっていた。表紙は黒、白、赤、灰色、緑があったが、表紙が緑のテスト冊子を使った学生たちは他の色の表紙の冊子を与えられた学生たちより創造的なアイデアを出すことができた。

　創造力を向上させるもう一つの方法は、心をさまよわせるための時間を定期的に作ることだ。散歩したり、窓の外を眺めたり、全く頭を使わない行為をしてみる。つまり、脳を休ませるのだ。それにより、意識が集中している時には思い浮かばなかったつながりを脳が作ることができる。休憩を取らないと、頭脳の創造力は引き出せない。だから、恐れずに問題を数分間忘れてみよう。そうすることが、問題の解決を見つける最良の方法になるかもしれないのだ。

True or False　解答 & 和訳

1. F　人は熱心に取り組まなければ、新しいアイデアを思いつくことはできない。
2. F　創造性は、完全に個性に拠る。
3. T　多くの良いアイデアは、他のことをしている時間に浮かぶ。
4. T　創造的なアイデアの思いつきは、何らかの形で色と結びついているかもしれない。
5. F　定期的に心をあそばせることは、創造性にとって悪い。
6. NS　心理学を学ぶことは、創造性を高める。

Unit 12

Playing at Work?
— 多様な場でのゲーミフィケーション —

computer game

phenomenon	名 現象		encouragement	名 励まし
gamification	名 ゲーミフィケーション		productivity	名 生産性
used to ~	かつて~していた		compliment	名 賛辞
influence	名 影響		supervisor	名 上司
stimulate	動 促進する		recognize	動 価値を認める
production	名 (化学物質の)生成		engage	動 引き込む
dopamine	名 ドーパミン (運動機能や認知機能などの中枢機能の調節に関与する伝達物質)		expert	名 専門家
			lead to ~	~につながる
involved	形 夢中になっている		evaluate	動 評価する
compete	動 競争する		definitely	副 確実に

12 速読

Playing at Work?

When people talk about games, they usually think of the board games or computer games people play for entertainment. However, there is a growing movement toward using games in new ways in the classroom, the workplace and other areas of society. This new phenomenon is called "gamification."

Some people used to believe that computer games had a bad effect on education. They believed that games had a bad influence on children's studies. However, scientists have found evidence that playing computer games can actually help the brain learn. Scientists have found that playing these games stimulates production of a chemical called dopamine. This chemical improves the ability to pay attention. Other research shows that the chance to gain some kind of reward increases the desire to do things. This encourages students to continue learning. By using games in the classroom, teachers can help students pay attention and stay involved.

Another area where "gamification" has an impact is the workplace. For example, some businesses have workers compete in games to lose weight and stay healthy. Competitors have a chance of winning material rewards and encouragement from coworkers. This can motivate workers to make healthy choices in eating or to continue exercising.

    Gamification also helps raise productivity. Some companies use online game systems to reward people for their achievements. Others reward workers for suggesting new ideas for products. The reward is not always money or a prize. It can be a compliment from a supervisor or other workers. Being recognized by others in the workplace motivates and engages workers.

    Experts have different views on the effects of gamification. Some say that it leads to unnecessary pressure and stress. Still, we see examples of gamification in areas of society people once would not have imagined. It may be necessary to evaluate the effects on a case-by-case basis. Each company, school, or organization includes different types of people. But it definitely looks like the use of games is now part of our everyday life.

332 words

12 True or False?

次の1～6の文を読み、本文の内容に合っていたらT、合わなかったらF、述べられていなかったらNS（Not stated）を選んでください。

1	Computer games are only used for entertainment.	T ☐ F ☐ NS ☐
2	Computer games cannot help the brain learn.	T ☐ F ☐ NS ☐
3	Dopamine can improve concentration and encourage learning.	T ☐ F ☐ NS ☐
4	Gamification can be used to encourage people to do exercise.	T ☐ F ☐ NS ☐
5	Those who play games at home perform well at work.	T ☐ F ☐ NS ☐
6	The effects of gamification should be evaluated individually.	T ☐ F ☐ NS ☐

スラッシュ訳

file-24

職場で遊ぶ
Playing at Work?

When people talk about games, / they usually think of / the board games / or computer games / people play for entertainment. // However, / there is a growing movement / toward using games / in new ways / in the classroom, the workplace and other areas of society. // This new phenomenon is called "gamification." //

Some people used to believe / that computer games had a bad effect / on education. // They believed / that games had a bad influence / on children's studies. // However, / scientists have found evidence / that playing computer games can actually help / the brain learn. // Scientists have found / that playing these games stimulates / production of a

12 スラッシュ訳

chemical / called dapamine.(ドーパミンと呼ばれる) // This chemical improves(この化学物質は能力を高める) the ability / to pay attention.(注意を払う) // Other research shows(別の研究は示す) / that the chance(機会が) / to gain some kind of reward(何らかの報酬を得る) / increases the desire(欲求を高める) / to do things.(何かすることに対する) // This encourages(これは生徒にやる気を起こさせる) students / to continue learning.(学習を続けることを) // By using games in the(教室内でゲームを使うことで) classroom, / teachers can help students(教師は生徒を助けることができる) / pay attention(集中して参加し続ける) and stay involved. //

Another area(別の分野は) / where "gamification" has an impact(「ゲーミフィケーション」が影響を及ぼしている) / is the workplace.(職場だ) // For example,(例えば) / some businesses(従業員に競争させる企業もある) have workers compete / in games(ゲームで) / to lose weight and(体重を減らし健康を維持するのを) stay healthy. // Competitors have a chance(参加者は機会を得る) / of winning(物質的な報酬と同僚からの励ましを勝ち取る) material rewards and encouragement from coworkers. // This can motivate workers(これは従業員のやる気を引き出すことができる) / to make healthy choices in(食事に関して健康的な選択をすること) eating / or to continue exercising.(または運動を続けることに対して) //

Gamification also helps raise productivity.(ゲーミフィケーションはまた生産性の向上を助ける) // Some(いくつかの) companies use online game systems(企業はオンラインゲームシステムを使う) / to reward people(人々に報酬を与えるのに)

124

for their achievements. // Others reward workers / for suggesting new ideas / for products. // The reward is not always money or a prize. // It can be a compliment / from a supervisor or other workers. // Being recognized / by others / in the workplace / motivates and engages workers. //

Experts have different views / on the effects of gamification. // Some say / that it leads / to unnecessary pressure and stress. // Still, / we see examples of gamification / in areas of society / people once would not have imagined. // It may be necessary / to evaluate the effects / on a case-by-case basis. // Each company, school, or organization / includes different types of people. // But / it definitely looks like / the use of games is now part of our everyday life. //

12 和訳 & 解答

職場で遊ぶとは

　人々がゲームについて話をする時、普通は娯楽のためにやるボードゲームやコンピュータゲームなどを思い浮かべる。しかし、教室や職場やその他社会の様々な領域で、ゲームの新しい利用法に対する動きが広まっている。この新しい現象は「ゲーミフィケーション」と呼ばれている。

　かつてコンピュータゲームは教育上良くないと考える人がいた。ゲームは子供たちの勉強に悪影響を与えると思われていたのだ。しかし実はそれどころか、コンピュータゲームは脳が学ぶことを助けるという証拠を科学者が発見した。ゲームをすることがドーパミンという化学物質の生成を促進することがわかったのだ。この化学物質は注意力を向上させる働きがある。他の研究では、何らかの報酬を得る機会があれば、やる気が増すことがわかった。これは、学生に勉強を継続させるように促す。教室内でゲームを使うことで、教師は学生が授業に集中し積極的に参加し続けるようにできる。

　「ゲーミフィケーション」が影響を与える他の分野は職場だ。たとえば一部の企業は、減量して健康な状態を保つことを従業員にゲームで競わせる。参加者は、賞品を獲得できたり、同僚からの励ましを受けたりする機会になる。それにより従業員は、食事の際に健康的な選択をしたり、運動を続けたりする気になれる。

　ゲーミフィケーションは、生産性の向上にも役立つ。オンラインのゲームシステムを使って従業員に業績に対する報酬を与える企業もあるし、製品の新しいアイデアを提案した従業員に報酬を与える企業もある。報酬は、必ずしもお金や賞品とは限らない。上司や他の同僚からの称賛であることもある。職場で周りに認められることは、従業員をやる気にさせ、仕事に熱中させる。

　ゲーミフィケーションの影響に関する見解は専門家によって異なる。それが不必要な圧力とストレスにつながるという意見もある。しかし、ゲーミフィケーションの例は、人々がかつて想像もしなかったような社会の分野に見られている。その影響は個別に判断する必要があるかもしれない。それぞれの企業、学校や団体は、異なる種類の人々を含んでいるからだ。しかし、ゲームの利用は、今や確実に我々の日常生活の一部に取り入れられているようだ。

True or False　解答 & 和訳

1. F　コンピュータゲームは、娯楽のためだけに使われる。
2. F　コンピュータゲームが、脳の学習を助けることはできない。
3. T　ドーパミンは、集中力を向上させ、学習効果を高める。
4. T　ゲーミフィケーションは、人々が運動するのを促すことができる。
5. NS　家でゲームをよくする人は、職場でよい仕事をする。
6. T　ゲーミフィケーションの効果は、個々に判断されるべきである。

Unit 13

Creating a Voice
― ボーカロイドと様々な可能性 ―

WATASHI HA VOCALOID DESU

voice synthesizing	音声合成	field	名 分野
composer	名 作曲家	medicine	名 医療
animated image	アニメの動画	generate	動 生む
cross	動 渡る	natural-sounding	形 自然に聞こえる
border	名 境	due to ~	~のため
poster girl	看板娘	neurological	形 神経的な
inspiration	名 創造性を刺激するもの	personalize	動 個人独自のものにする
attract	動 魅了する	express	動 表す
stimulate	動 刺激する	pass away	亡くなる
advanced	形 先進の	pleasant	形 心地よい

13 速読

Creating a Voice

　Voice-synthesizing technology has made it possible to create digital characters who can talk and sing. One advantage of such software is that anyone can use a computer to create music and words for songs. Almost anyone can become a music composer and producer. Some people add animated images to their original songs. They can put their own music videos on the Web. Some are lucky enough to gain enough popularity to make a commercial recording. The popularity of this software has crossed national and industry borders.

　Hatsune Miku is the poster girl of this new techology. She is the inspiration for a manga series as well as for games and clothing. She has also attracted fans from around the world to concerts. At these concerts 3D images are shown on a screen on a stage. This new development has stimulated networks of "creators." People living in different parts of the world work together to create new songs and performances.

　Advanced voice-synthesizing technology has gone beyond the entertainment industry. It is creating possibilities in fields such as medicine. The technology can generate natural-sounding human voices. Researchers make a database of voice samples where the pitch, tone and speed can be changed. They can create a voice for people who have difficulties speaking. They can also give a voice to people who have lost their voice due to neurological problems. The personalized voice can be used to produce words and express feelings. This improves communication and the person's quality of life. It provides the person with a sense of individual identity.

There are other ways in which voice-synthesizing technology can be used. For example, it is possible to record new songs by singers who have already passed away. It is also possible to create pleasant computerized voices to give instructions over the phone.

We once thought it would be a long time before humans would live together with androids that speak to us in human voices. But that reality is already here.

333 words

13 True or False?

次の1〜6の文を読み、本文の内容に合っていたらT、合わなかったらF、述べられていなかったらNS (Not stated) を選んでください。

---

1. Special software lets anyone compose music.

   T ☐
   F ☐
   NS ☐

---

2. Voice-synthesizing software is found only in Japan.

   T ☐
   F ☐
   NS ☐

---

3. Images of Hatsune Miku can be shown in 3D on a stage.

   T ☐
   F ☐
   NS ☐

---

4. Technology provides a synthetic voice for people who have lost their natural voice.

   T ☐
   F ☐
   NS ☐

---

5. Personalized voices are impossible to create.

   T ☐
   F ☐
   NS ☐

---

6. Androids are able to compose songs by themselves.

   T ☐
   F ☐
   NS ☐

スラッシュ訳

声を作る
Creating a Voice

音声合成技術はそれを可能にした
Voice-synthesizing technology has made it possible / to create digital characters / who can talk and sing. // One advantage of such software is / that anyone can use a computer / to create music and words for songs. // Almost anyone can become / a music composer and producer. // Some people add animated images / to their original songs. // They can put their own music videos / on the Web. // Some are lucky enough / to gain enough popularity / to make a commercial recording. / The popularity of this software / has crossed national and industry borders. //

Hatsune Miku is the poster girl / of this new technology. // She is the inspiration for a manga series / as well as for games and clothing. // She has

13 スラッシュ訳

ファンを集めた / 世界中から /
also attracted fans / from around the world / to

コンサートへ // これらのコンサートでは / 3Dの動画が映される /
concerts. // At these concerts / 3D images are shown /

ステージ上のスクリーンに // この新しい発展は /
on a screen on a stage. // This new development / has

「クリエイター」のネットワークを活性化した // 世界の離れた場所に
stimulated networks of "creators." // People living in

住んでいる人たちが / 協力する / 新しい歌と演
different parts of the world / work together / to create

奏を作り出すために //
new songs and performances. //

最新の音声合成技術は / 娯楽産業の範
Advanced voice-synthesizing technology / has gone

囲を越えた // それは可能性を
beyond the entertainment industry. // It is creating

生み出している / 医療などの分野で
possibilities / in fields such as medicine. // The

その技術は作り出すことができる / 自然に聞こえる人間の声を
technology can generate / natural-sounding human

// 研究者はデータベースを作る / 声の
voices. // Researchers make a database / of voice

サンプルの / 音の高さ、声の調子、そしてスピードを変えることができる
samples / where the pitch, tone and speed can be

// 彼らは声を作ることができる / 話をするのが困難な人の
changed. // They can create a voice / for people who

ために / 彼らはまた声を与えることができる /
have difficulties speaking. // They can also give a voice /

声を失った人に / 神経系の
to people who have lost their voice / due to

問題により // 個人仕様に変えられた声が使われることが
neurological problems. // The personalized voice can

be used / to produce words / and express feelings. //
This improves / communication and the person's quality of life. // It provides the person / with a sense of individual identity. //

There are other ways / in which voice-synthesizing technology can be used. / For example, / it is possible / to record new songs / by singers who have already passed away. // It is also possible / to create pleasant computerized voices / to give instructions / over the phone. //

We once thought / it would be a long time / before humans would live together with androids / that speak to us in human voices. // But that reality is already here. //

13 和訳 & 解答

声をつくる

　音声合成技術により、話したり歌ったりできるデジタルキャラクターをつくることが可能になった。このようなソフトの利点のひとつは、誰でもコンピューターで歌詞と曲がつくれることだ。ほぼ誰もが作曲家兼音楽プロデューサーになれる。オリジナル曲にアニメをつける人々もいる。彼らはウェブ上に自分の音楽ビデオをアップできる。幸運にも営利目的のレコーディングをするほどの人気を得る人々もいる。このソフトは、国や業界の垣根を越えて人気を得ている。

　初音ミクは、この新技術の看板娘だ。ゲームや衣服に加えてマンガのシリーズもなっている。コンサートには世界中からファンも集った。コンサートではステージ上のスクリーンに3D動画が映し出される。この新たな展開は、「クリエイター」のネットワークを活性化した。世界各地の人々が協力して、新しい歌やパフォーマンスを生みだしている。

　高度な音声合成技術は、娯楽産業の範囲を越えて、医療などの分野に可能性をもたらしている。この技術は、自然な人間の声をつくり出せる。研究者は、声の高さや調子、速さを変えられる声のサンプルのデータベースを作っており、発話障害のある人々のために声をつくることができる。また、神経的な障害のために声を失った人々に声を与えることもできる。個人仕様に変えられた声は、言葉を発して感情を表現するために使われる。これは意思の疎通と生活の質の向上につながり、人々に個人のアイデンティティーの感覚を与えてくれる。

　音声合成技術を利用できる方法は他にもある。たとえば、すでに亡くなった歌手の声で新曲のレコーディングができる。また、電話の音声ガイダンス用に耳に心地よいコンピューター音声も作ることができる。

　かつては、人間の声で話すアンドロイドが人類と共存する時代はまだまだ先のことであると思われていた。しかし、その現実はすでに始まっているのだ。

True or False　解答 & 和訳

1. T　特別なソフトウェアによって、誰にでも音楽を作ることができる。
2. F　音声合成ソフトは、日本でしか手に入らない。
3. T　初音ミクの画像は、ステージで3D映像として見せることができる。
4. T　生来の声を失った人たちに合成音声を提供するのは技術的に可能だ。
5. F　個人独自の声は、作ることはできない。
6. NS　アンドロイドは、自ら歌を作曲することができる。

Unit 14

To Like or Not to Like
— 味覚と好き嫌い —

particular	形 特別な	fancy	形 高級な
exposure	名 さらされること	ordinary	形 普通の
the more ~, the more ~	~をすればするほど~になる	impressed	形 感銘を受けた
consumer	名 消費者	emotion	名 感情
tend to ~	~する傾向がある	affect	動 影響を与える
get tired of ~	~に飽きる	remind	動 思い起こさせる
factor	名 要因	warmth	名 温かさ
describe	動 説明する	energetic	形 活力に満ちた
description	名 説明	preference	名 好み
ironic	形 皮肉な、偶然の	breast-feed	動 母乳を与える

14 速読

To Like or Not to Like

Several things are true about the tastes we like and don't like. Although people can tell you what foods they like, they are not always able to tell *why* they like those foods. Secondly, if people have not tried a certain kind of food, they probably think they won't like it.

People often like a particular food because they have repeated exposure to it. Generally speaking, the more times you try something, the more you will like it. With young children, for example, it usually takes about nine exposures before they begin to like something.

As a person grows older, he or she learns to like more complex tastes. Consumers tend to get tired of single flavors, such as an orange drink, rather quickly. If they have one bottle, they probably will not drink a second bottle. Colas have more complex flavors, so they may drink a second bottle.

Why do we choose certain kinds of foods? In a restaurant, naming is an important factor. If the menu uses Italian words in describing a dish and we have enjoyed Italian food before, we may select that dish because of the description. In other words, it "sounds good."

The reason we like something is often ironic. For example, if you are in a fancy restaurant, you will think the food is better. If the wine comes from France, you will think it is better. If the food and wine are in an ordinary café, you may not be impressed.

Mood and emotion also affect whether you like something. In the morning, cinnamon appeals to you because it reminds you of baking and warmth. This is a good way to start the day. Later in the day, you might prefer red pepper because it is active and energetic.

Perhaps more than anything else, a mother's diet influences preferences of a child. For example, if a mother drinks carrot juice before her baby is born or while she is breast-feeding her baby, the baby will tend to like carrots.

342 words

14 True or False?

次の 1 ～ 6 の文を読み、本文の内容に合っていたら T、合わなかったら F、述べられていなかったら NS（Not stated）を選んでください。

1	If a person has not tried a food, he probably thinks he won't like it.	T ☐ F ☐ NS ☐
2	Children need to try a food repeatedly before they begin to like it.	T ☐ F ☐ NS ☐
3	Adults generally like food with just one flavor.	T ☐ F ☐ NS ☐
4	Using an Italian word to describe a dish on a menu raises the price.	T ☐ F ☐ NS ☐
5	Our preferences for tastes may depend on the time of day.	T ☐ F ☐ NS ☐
6	A baby's preferences can be influenced by the mother's diet.	T ☐ F ☐ NS ☐

スラッシュ訳

好きになるか、ならないか
To Like or Not to Like

いくつかの事は真実だ / 味に関する / 我々が好
Several things are true / about the tastes / we like
きと好きではない // 人々は言うことができるが
and don't like. // Although people can tell you / what
どの食べ物が好きか / 彼らはいつも言えるわけではない /
foods they like, / they are not always able to tell /
なぜそれらの食べ物が好きか // 二つ目に / もし人が試した
why they like those foods. // Secondly, / if people
ことがない場合 / ある種の食べ物 / 彼らはおそらく思う
have not tried / a certain kind of food, / they probably
であろう / それは好きではないだろう //
think / they won't like it. //

人はよくある特定の食べ物を好む / なぜならそれに繰り
People often like a particular food / because they
返し触れてきたからだ // 一般的に /
have repeated exposure to it. // Generally speaking, /
何かを食べる回数が増えれば増えるほど / それがより好きになる
the more times you try something, / the more you will
幼児においては / 例えば /
like it. // With young children, / for example, / it
通常9回くらい触れる必要がある / 何かを好きになる
usually takes about nine exposures / before they
前に
begin to like something. //

人は歳をとるにしたがって / その人は好きになることを覚える /
As a person grows older, / he or she learns to like /
より複雑な味を // 消費者は傾向がある / ひとつの味
more complex tastes. // Consumers tend to / get tired

14 スラッシュ訳

of single flavors, / such as an orange drink, / rather
quickly. // If they have one bottle, / they probably will
not drink a second bottle. // Colas have more complex
flavors, / so they may drink a second bottle. //

Why do we choose certain kinds of foods? // In a
restaurant, / naming is an important factor. // If the
menu uses Italian words / in describing a dish / and we
have enjoyed Italian food before, / we may select that
dish / because of the description. // In other words, / it
"sounds good." //

The reason we like something / is often ironic. // For
example, / if you are in a fancy restaurant, / you will
think the food is better. // If the wine comes from
France, / you will think it is better. // If the food and
wine are in an ordinary café, / you may not be
impressed. //

Mood and emotion also affect / whether you like something. // In the morning, / cinnamon appeals to you / because it reminds you of baking and warmth. // This is a good way / to start the day. // Later in the day, / you might prefer red pepper / because it is active and energetic. //

Perhaps more than anything else, / a mother's diet influences / preferences of a child. // For example, / if a mother drinks carrot juice / before her baby is born / or while she is breast-feeding her baby, / the baby will tend to like carrots. //

14 和訳 & 解答

好きになるか、ならないか

　人間の味の好き嫌いについて言えることがいくつかある。人は自分がどんな食べ物が好きかは言えるけれども、好きな理由が説明できるとは限らない。また人は、食べたことがない物は、食べても好みにあわないだろうと思うことが多い。

　人は、食べなれているという理由で食べ物を好むことが多い。大抵は食べた回数に応じて好きになっていく。たとえば幼児は、ある食べ物を好きになり始めるまでに通常9回くらい食べる必要がある。

　人は年をとるにつれ、より複雑な味を好むようになる。消費者は、オレンジ飲料のような単一の味にはかなり早くあきる傾向がある。ビン1本を飲めば、おそらく続けてもう1本は飲まないだろう。コーラはより複雑な味なので、2本目を飲むかもしれない。

　我々がある種の食べ物を選ぶ理由はなんだろうか。レストランでは命名は大事な要素だ。もしメニューで料理の説明にイタリア語の単語が使われていたら、以前にイタリア料理を堪能したことがある人は、その説明が理由でその料理を選ぶかもしれない。つまり、それが「よさそうな響き」だからだ。

　人が何かを好む理由は偶然なことも多い。たとえば人は高級レストランにいると食べ物がよりおいしいと思う。ワインがフランス産だとよりおいしいと思う。ありふれた食堂で同じ料理とワインが出てきても、たいして感心はしない。

　気分や感情も好みに影響を及ぼす。朝、シナモンを好ましく感じるのは、パンを焼くことや暖かい感じを連想させるからだ。これは1日の始まりにはふさわしい。もっと遅い時間帯には、活動的で活力に富む赤唐辛子のほうを好むかもしれない。

　そしておそらく他の何よりも母親の食生活は、子どもの好き嫌いに影響する。例えば母親が、出産前かまたは授乳期間中にニンジンのジュースを飲んでいると、子どもはニンジンが好きになる傾向がある。

True or False　解答 & 和訳

1. T 　人がある食物を食べたことがない場合、おそらくそれを好きではないと思うだろう。
2. T 　子どもたちは、その食べ物を好きになる前に、繰り返し食べる必要がある。
3. F 　大人は、一般的に単一の味の食物を好む。
4. NS　イタリアの言葉をメニューで料理に使うことによって、価格が上がる。
5. T 　私たちの味の好みは、一日の時間帯に拠っている。
6. T 　子どもの味の好みは、母親が日常食べる物に影響されている。

Unit 15

3D Printing
— 3Dプリンターとその可能性 —

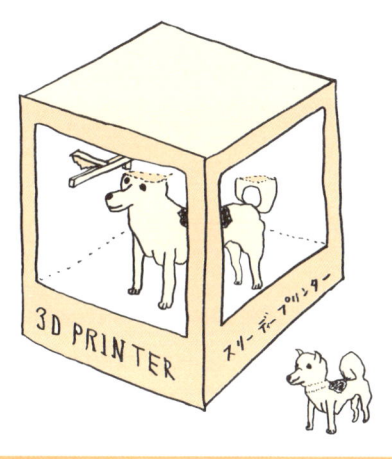

design	動 設計する	decoration	名 装飾
three-dimensional	形 3次元の	figure	名 フィギュア
layer	名 層	incident	名 事件
light-sensitive	形 感光性の	various	形 様々な
include	動 含む	try out	使ってみる
liquid	名 液体	redesign	動 設計し直す
titanium	名 チタン(軽い金属、元素記号Ti)	improvement	名 改善
combination	名 組み合わせ	produce	動 作る
individual	名 個人	medical	形 医療の
jewelry	名 宝飾品類	replace	動 置き換える

15 速読

3D Printing

Designing new products has just become a lot easier. A designer can now use special software to make a three-dimensional (3D) design on a computer. The computer then sends the data to a special kind of printer called a 3D printer. That printer makes a copy of the computer model with layer after layer of light-sensitive material. These materials can include liquids, plastics, titanium, and even paper. Some 3D printers use a combination of these materials.

In the beginning, these printers were large and very expensive, so only companies could buy them. But now small printers are selling for lower prices, so individuals are using them in hobbies. People are using them to create things like jewelry, decorations, toys, and figures. Other people are using a computer to design unique cases for iPhones, producing copies with 3D printers, and selling those cases on the Internet. Serious amateurs use these printers to make bicycles and even guitars. A recent dramatic incident reported in the news was a case where someone created plastic guns with a printer. The guns actually worked.

Round 1	Round 2	Round 3	Round 4	Round 5	Round 6
WPM 語	WPM 語	WPM 語	WPM 語	WPM 語	WPM 語
月 日	月 日	月 日	月 日	月 日	月 日

Various industries are already using these printers to create test parts that go into cars, airplanes, and machinery. Using a 3D printer is much cheaper than making an actual part by traditional methods. It is possible to make an item, try it out, and then redesign it and reprint it. Other methods may take several days or weeks. A 3D printer, however, makes it possible to redesign and print several times in the same day. This lets the designer make improvements very quickly.

These new printers are already used to produce models of houses and buildings. They are also used to produce 3D maps of cities, mountains, and rivers. They are also beginning to be used in medical fields. With special materials, it is possible to create bones, ears and noses to replace a broken body part. If a bone is broken, a doctor may one day print a 3D copy to replace it.

336 words

15 True or False?

次の1～6の文を読み、本文の内容に合っていたらT、合わなかったらF、述べられていなかったらNS（Not stated）を選んでください。

1	3D design software can be used on any computer.	T ☐ F ☐ NS ☐
2	The materials used in 3D printing include plastic and paper.	T ☐ F ☐ NS ☐
3	Individuals can now buy printers to use in hobbies.	T ☐ F ☐ NS ☐
4	Manufacturers of car parts use printers to test designs.	T ☐ F ☐ NS ☐
5	3D printers take one day to produce an item.	T ☐ F ☐ NS ☐
6	Models of mountains and rivers can be produced with this software.	T ☐ F ☐ NS ☐

スラッシュ訳

file-30

3D 印刷
3D Printing

Designing new products / has just become a lot easier. // A designer can now use special software / to make a three-dimensional (3D) design / on a computer. // The computer then sends the data / to a special kind of printer / called a 3D printer. // That printer makes a copy / of the computer model / with layer after layer / of light-sensitive material. // These materials can include / liquids, plastics, titanium, and even paper. // Some 3D printers use a combination of these materials. //

In the beginning, / these printers were large and very expensive, / so only companies could buy them. // But now small printers are selling / for lower prices, / so individuals are using them / in hobbies. // People

15 スラッシュ訳

are using them / to create things / like jewelry,
_{それらを使っている} / _{物を作るために} / _{宝飾品、装飾品、}

decorations, toys, and figures. // Other people are using
_{玩具、そしてフィギュアなどの} // _{他の人たちはコンピューターを}

a computer / to design unique cases for iPhones, /
_{使っている} / _{ユニークな iPhone のケースをデザインするのに}

producing copies with 3D printers, / and selling those
_{3D プリンターで複製を作って} / _{そしてネット上で}

cases on the Internet. // Serious amateurs use these
_{それらのケースを販売する} // _{入れ込んでいる素人はそれらのプリンターを}

printers / to make bicycles and even guitars. // A recent
_{使う} / _{自転車やギターさえも作るのに} // _{最近の印象}

dramatic incident / reported in the news / was a case /
_{的な出来事は} / _{ニュースで報道された} / _{事件だった}

where someone created plastic guns with a printer. //
_{誰かがプリンターを使ってプラスチックの銃を作った}

The guns actually worked. //
_{銃は実際に機能した}

Various industries are already using these printers /
_{様々な産業はこれらのプリンターをもうすでに使っている}

to create test parts / that go into cars, airplanes, and
_{試作部品を作るのに} / _{車、飛行機、機械に組み込まれる}

machinery. // Using a 3D printer is much cheaper / than
_{3D プリンターを使うと費用が大分安い}

making an actual part / by traditional methods. // It is
_{実際の部品を作るよりも} / _{従来の方法で} // _{それは}

possible / to make an item, / try it out, / and then
_{可能だ} / _{物を作る} / _{それを試す} / _{それから}

redesign it / and reprint it. // Other methods may take
_{設計し直す} / _{プリントし直す} // _{他の方法では数日または数週間かかる}

several days or weeks. // A 3D printer, / however, /
_{かもしれない} // _{3D プリンターは} / _{しかし}

makes it possible / to redesign and print several times / in the same day. // This lets the designer / make improvements / very quickly. //
These new printers are already used / to produce models / of houses and buildings. // They are also used / to produce 3D maps / of cities, mountains, and rivers. // They are also beginning to be used / in medical fields. // With special materials, / it is possible / to create bones, ears and noses / to replace a broken body part. // If a bone is broken, / a doctor may one day print a 3D copy / to replace it. //

15 和訳 & 解答

3D 印刷

　最近、新製品の設計はずいぶんと楽にできるようになった。今や設計者は、専用のソフトを使ってコンピュータで3次元（3D）デザインを作ることができる。コンピュータは次に、3Dプリンターと呼ばれる特殊なプリンターにデータを送る。プリンターは、感光性の材料を何層にも重ねていくことでコンピュータのモデルのコピーを作る。材料には、液体、プラスチック、チタンや紙まである。これらの複数の材料を組み合わせて使用する3Dプリンターもある。

　当初はこれらのプリンターは大型で非常に高価だったため、企業しか購入できなかった。しかし現在は、小型のプリンターが手頃な価格になってきているので、個人が趣味で使っている。人々はプリンターを使って、宝飾品、装飾品、玩具やフィギュアなどを作っている。コンピューターで独自のiPhoneケースをデザインし、3Dプリンターでコピーをつくってインターネット上で販売している人々もいる。熱心なアマチュアは、これらのプリンターで自転車やギターまでも製造する。最近のニュースで、プリンターでプラスチック銃を製造した人間がいるという印象的な事件が報道された。銃は実際に使用できた。

　様々な産業が、すでにこれらのプリンターを使用して、車、飛行機や機械のための試作部品を作製している。立体3Dプリンターを使用した方が、従来の方法よりずっと安上がりなのだ。製品を作り、試用して、それからデザインを変更して再びプリントアウトすることが可能だ。他の方法だと数日から数週間もかかりかねないが、3Dプリンターなら一日のうちにデザインの変更とプリントアウトを何度もすることができる。これにより設計者は迅速に製品を改良することができる。

　これらの新しいプリンターは、すでに家やビルの模型を作るのに用いられている。さらにこれらを使って、都市や山や川の立体地図が作られている。医療分野でも使用され始めていて、特別な材料を使って、損傷した体の一部のかわりとなる骨、耳や鼻を作ることができる。将来、骨折したら医者が交換用の3Dの複製をプリントアウトする日が来るかもしれない。

True or False　解答 & 和訳

1. NS　3Dデザインソフトは、どんなコンピュータでも使える。
2. T　3Dプリンターで使われる材料には、プラスチックや紙も含まれる。
3. T　今や、個人が趣味で使うためにプリンターを買うことができる。
4. T　自動車部品の製造業者は、設計案を試すためにプリンターを使う。
5. F　3Dプリンターは、ひとつの品をつくるのに1日かかる。
6. T　山や川の模型を、このソフトウェアでつくり出すことができる。

Unit 16

Give Them a Hand
― 左利きについての一考察 ―

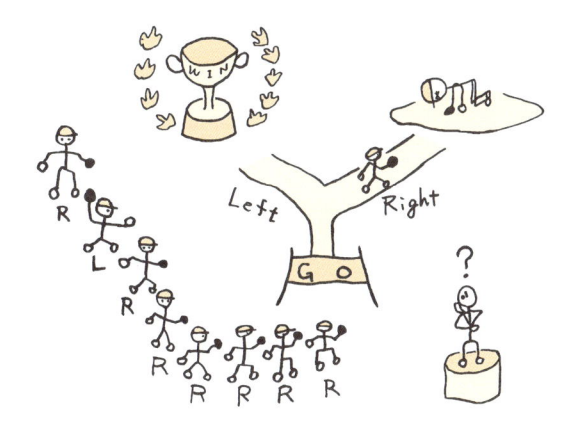

give ~ a hand	～を手助けする	allow	動 許す
preference	名 優先傾向	whichever	代 どちらの～でも
left-handed	形 左利きの	used to ~	かつて～した
suffer	動 苦しむ	scissor	名 (通常scissors)はさみ
right-handed	形 右利きの	situation	名 状況
struggle	動 苦労する	advantage	名 強み
force	動 強制する	be used to ~ing	～するのに慣れている
punish	動 罰を与える	advantageous	形 有利な
fortunately	副 幸いにも	batting	名 (野球の)打撃
accept	動 受け入れる	share	動 共有する

16 速読

Give Them a Hand

The human preference for using the right or left hand has long been a mystery to scientists. Wouldn't it be more natural if everyone used both hands or if half used the right and half used the left? Actually, only one in ten people are left-handed.

Until the late 20th century, left-handed people suffered in various ways. In schools, chairs with desks were made to be convenient for right-handed people. Left-handed people struggled when they used these desks. Some parents and teachers forced left-handed children to change to the right hand. Sometimes these children were punished if they used their left hand for writing or eating.

Fortunately, left-handedness has become more accepted. Children are usually allowed to use whichever hand they choose. Left-handed people used to struggle to use right-handed tools. Now, designers produce specially designed tools, such as knives and scissors, for people who prefer to use their left hand.

In some situations, being left-handed can even be an advantage. In several sports, left-handedness seems to be an advantage. In sports such as table tennis, boxing, baseball and basketball, right-handers are used to competing against other right-handers. When they compete against left-handers, the left-hander has the advantage of surprise. Some 30% of top-level baseball players are left-handed. Hideki Matsui and Ichiro Suzuki showed how advantageous this is when batting. It is even more of an advantage in basketball, where over half of the top players are left-handed.

Being left-handed is not always an advantage, though. In golf, for example, the number of left-handed top-level players is very small. This is probably because it is hard to find left-handed golf clubs.

Why is there such a strong tendency for people to be right-handed? Maybe humans learned to both cooperate and compete with one another. They cooperated by sharing tools. Therefore, it was better if most people used the same hand. But in competition, in battle or in sports, the left-handed person had an advantage. In our world, we balance competition with cooperation, so perhaps we need a few left-handers and a larger group of right-handers.

349 words

16 True or False?

次の1〜6の文を読み、本文の内容に合っていたらT、合わなかったらF、述べられていなかったらNS（Not stated）を選んでください。

1	Twenty percent of humans are left-handed.	T ☐ F ☐ NS ☐
2	Some children were forced to write with their right hand.	T ☐ F ☐ NS ☐
3	Tools can be designed for left-handed people.	T ☐ F ☐ NS ☐
4	Being left-handed is an advantage in all sports.	T ☐ F ☐ NS ☐
5	Good players can use either hand equally well.	T ☐ F ☐ NS ☐
6	Both competition and cooperation are important to humans.	T ☐ F ☐ NS ☐

スラッシュ訳

彼らに手を貸そう
Give Them a Hand

The human human preference ／ for using the right or left hand ／ has long been a mystery ／ to scientists. ∥ Wouldn't it be more natural ／ if everyone used both hands ／ or if half used the right ／ and half used the left? ∥ Actually, only one in ten people are left-handed. ∥

Until the late 20th century, ／ left-handed people suffered ／ in various ways. ∥ In schools, ／ chairs with desks were made ／ to be convenient for right-handed people. ∥ Left-handed people struggled ／ when they used these desks. ∥ Some parents and teachers forced ／ left-handed children to change ／ to the right hand. ∥ Sometimes these children were punished ／ if they used their left hand ／ for writing or eating. ∥

16 スラッシュ訳

Fortunately, / left-handedness has become more accepted. // Children are usually allowed / to use / whichever hand they choose. // Left-handed people used to struggle / to use right-handed tools. // Now, / designers produce / specially designed tools, / such as knives and scissors, / for people / who prefer to use their left hand. //

In some situations, / being left-handed can even be an advantage. // In several sports, / left-handedness seems to be an advantage. // In sports / such as table tennis, boxing, baseball and basketball, / right-handers are used to competing / against other right-handers. // When they compete against left-handers, / the left-hander has the advantage / of surprise. // Some 30% of top-level baseball players / are left-handed. // Hideki Matsui and Ichiro Suzuki showed / how advantageous this is when batting. It is even more of an advantage in basketball, where over half of the top players are left-handed.

Being left-handed is not always an advantage, though. In golf, for example, the number of left-handed top-level players is very small. This is probably because it is hard to find left-handed golf clubs.

Why is there such a strong tendency for people to be right-handed? Maybe humans learned to both cooperate and compete with one another. They cooperated by sharing tools. Therefore, it was better if most people used the same hand. But in competition, in battle or in sports, the left-handed person had an advantage. In our world, we balance competition with cooperation, so perhaps we need a few left-handers and a larger group of right-handers.

16 和訳 & 解答

彼らに手を貸そう

　人間の左右の利き手に関する優先傾向は、科学者にとって長年の謎であった。皆が両手を使うか、または、右手と左手を使う人が半々であるほうが自然ではないだろうか。しかし実際は、左利きは10人に1人しかいない。

　20世紀後半までは、左利きの人々は苦労した。学校の机つきの椅子は右利き用に作られていたので、左利きの人々はこの机を使うのに苦労した。親や教師が左利きの子どもを無理に右利きに矯正したこともあり、左利きの子どもが書いたり食べたりする時に左手を使うと罰を受けることもあった。

　幸い左利きは受け入れられるようになってきた。子どもたちは大抵、好きなほうの手を使うことを許されている。左利きの人々は、かつては右利き用の道具を使うのに苦労してきたが、現在では設計者はナイフやはさみなど左利き用に特別に設計された道具を作っている。

　左利きであることが有利な場合さえある。いくつかのスポーツでは、左利きは有利であるようだ。卓球、ボクシング、野球やバスケットボールのようなスポーツでは、右利きの人々は対戦相手も右利きであることに慣れているので、左利きと対戦する時には、左利きが不意をつけるので有利なのだ。トップレベルの野球選手のおよそ3割は左利きである。松井秀喜選手とイチロー選手は左利きが打撃の際にいかに有利であるか示している。バスケットボールにおいて、左利きはさらに有利で、トッププレーヤーの過半数が左利きである。

　左利きがいつでも有利というわけではない。例えばゴルフでは、左利きのトップレベルのプレーヤーは非常に少ない。これはおそらく、左利き用のクラブがなかなか手に入らないからだろう。

　なぜ、右利きに対する強い優先傾向があるのだろうか。人間は、お互いに協力することと競争することの両方を学んだのかもしれない。そして道具を共有することで、協力し合った。したがって、ほとんどの人が同じ利き手を使ったほうが都合が良かったのだ。しかし競技会や戦いやスポーツでは、左利きのほうに分があった。今日の世界では、人は競争と協力とのバランスをとっているので、おそらく、少数の左利きと、多数の右利きが必要なのだろう。

True or False　解答 & 和訳

1. F　人の20パーセントは左利きだ。
2. T　かつては、右手で書くように矯正させられる子どももいた。
3. T　左利き用の道具を設計することができる。
4. F　左利きの人はすべてのスポーツにおいて有利である。
5. NS　優れたプレーヤーはどちらの手も器用に使うことができる。
6. T　競争と協力はどちらも人間にとって大切である。

Unit 17

Education for What?
— 夢と教育、そして自己思考力 —

business	名 企業		succeed	動 成功する
employee	名 従業員		qualified	形 適性のある
schooling	名 学校教育		applicant	名 応募者
along the way	その途中で		graduation	名 卒業
lost	形 戸惑った		solid	形 確かな
extremely	副 きわめて		devote	動 捧げる
fill in	記入する		broaden	動 拡げる
application	名 応募書類		a wide variety of ~	多様な~
rarely	副 めったに~ない		critically	副 批判的に
unfilled	形 満たされていない		liberal arts	教養科目
encourage	動 奨励する		potential	形 潜在的な

17 速読

Education for What?

There seems to be a gap between the jobs that people seek and the jobs that companies actually offer. The result is that job-hunters cannot find work and businesses cannot find employees. This is happening around the world.

Parents and teachers have long told children, "Follow your dreams." So, students focus first on getting into the next level of schooling and second on doing what they find interesting. Along the way, they usually do their best to avoid the difficult subjects in school, unless those subjects are on the entrance examinations. Once students get into university, they are a little bit lost. This is because they have reached their "goal" of passing the entrance examination. They do not have a clear idea of what to do during the next four years. As the third year comes around, they once again try to "follow their dreams" by looking for jobs at extremely competitive companies. They fill in dozens of applications and wait for a call from the company inviting them to come for an interview. That phone call rarely comes.

There are jobs, however, in small and medium-size

companies. There are also jobs in the STEM fields that go unfilled. STEM stands for Science, Technology, Engineering and Mathematics. Governments and businesses are making efforts to encourage students to take interest in these fields beginning in elementary school. If these efforts succeed, there will be more qualified applicants for jobs after graduation from university. For those looking for jobs in these fields it will be easier to find jobs. For the companies, it will be easier to hire employees with a solid background.

But is the real goal of university education to provide employees? Many say that one's university years should be devoted to broadening one's view of the world. Some say that students should spend more time reading a wide variety of books. Others say that students should learn how to think critically. In other words, they should focus on liberal arts so that they can develop the ability to think for themselves. University should train the individual, not train a potential employee.

355 words

17 True or False?

次の1〜6の文を読み、本文の内容に合っていたらT、合わなかったらF、述べられていなかったらNS（Not stated）を選んでください。

1. Around the world, there is a gap between jobs and job-hunters.
   - T ☐
   - F ☐
   - NS ☐

2. Some students focus only on passing entrance exams.
   - T ☐
   - F ☐
   - NS ☐

3. Most students know what to do during their university years.
   - T ☐
   - F ☐
   - NS ☐

4. Some small companies cannot find employees to work for them.
   - T ☐
   - F ☐
   - NS ☐

5. Students are encouraged to take courses in STEM fields.
   - T ☐
   - F ☐
   - NS ☐

6. All job-hunters should get a university education.
   - T ☐
   - F ☐
   - NS ☐

スラッシュ訳

Education for What?
何のための教育か

There seems to be a gap / between / the jobs that people seek / and the jobs that companies actually offer. // The result is / that job-hunters cannot find work / and businesses cannot find employees. // This is happening / around the world. //

Parents and teachers have long told children, / "Follow your dreams." // So, students focus first on / getting into the next level of schooling / and second on doing what they find interesting. // Along the way, / they usually do their best / to avoid the difficult subjects / in school, / unless those subjects are on the entrance examinations. // Once students get into university, / they are a little bit lost. // This is because / they have reached their "goal" / of passing the

17　スラッシュ訳

entrance examination. // _{彼らははっきりした考えを持てない} They do not have a clear idea / _{何をすれば良いかという} of what to do / _{次の4年間} during the next four years. // _{3年目が巡って} As the third _{くると} year comes around, / _{彼らはもう一度しようとする} they once again try / _{「彼らの夢を追う」ことを} to "follow their dreams" / _{仕事を探すことで} by looking for jobs / _{きわめて競争の激しい企業において} at extremely competitive companies. // _{彼らは何十もの応募書類に記入する} They fill in dozens of applications / _{そして電話を待つ} and wait for a call / _{会社からの} from the company / _{面接に来るようにという連絡を} inviting them to come for an interview. // _{そのような電話はめったに来ない} That phone call rarely comes. //

_{仕事はある} There are jobs, / _{しかし} however, / _{中小企業で} in small and medium-size companies. // _{仕事はまたある} There are also jobs / _{STEM分野で} in the STEM fields / _{満たされないままになっている} that go unfilled. // _{STEMは意味する} STEM stands for / _{科学、} Science, _{技術、工業、数学} Technology, Engineering and Mathematics. //

_{政府と企業は努力をしている} Governments and businesses are making efforts / to _{生徒に奨励する} encourage students / _{興味を持つことを} to take interest / _{これらの分野で} in these fields / _{小学校から始まる} beginning in elementary school. // _{もしこれらの試みが成功したら} If these efforts succeed, / _{適格な応募者が増える} there will be more qualified applicants / _{仕事} for

jobs / after graduation from university. // For those looking for jobs / in these fields / it will be easier to find jobs. // For the companies, / it will be easier to hire employees / with a solid background. //

But is the real goal of university education / to provide employees? // Many say / that one's university years should be devoted / to broadening one's view of the world. // Some say / that students should spend more time / reading a wide variety of books. // Others say / that students should learn / how to think critically. // In other words, / they should focus on liberal arts / so that they can develop the ability / to think for themselves. // University should train the individual, / not train a potential employee. //

17 和訳 & 解答

何のための教育か

　人々がやりたがる仕事と、企業が実際に求人する仕事との間にギャップがあるようだ。そのために、求職者は仕事を見つけられず、企業は従業員を見つけられない。これは世界中で起こっている。

　親や教師は、ずっと子どもたちに「夢を追いなさい」と言い聞かせてきた。だから学生たちは、まずは進学していくことを第一に考え、その次に自分が興味のあることを考える。その過程において大抵は、受験に関係ない限り難しい科目はなんとかして避けようとする。一旦大学に入ると、彼らは少々戸惑う。なぜなら、入試に合格するという「ゴール」に達したからだ。彼らにはそれからの4年間で何をするという明確な考えがない。3年生になると、彼らは競争率の非常に高い会社に就職しようとすることで、もう一度「夢を追う」ことを試みる。何十社も応募して、企業から面接の連絡の電話が来るのを待つが、そのような電話はめったに来ない。

　しかし、中小企業になら仕事はある。STEMの分野にも空きはある。STEMとは、Science（科学）、Technology（テクノロジー）、Engineering（エンジニアリング）、Mathematics（数学）の略。政府と企業は、生徒たちに小学校からこれらの分野に興味を持たせようと努力している。これらの努力が実を結べば、仕事に適格な新卒の求職者が増えることになる。これらの分野で仕事を探す求職者は採用されやすいだろう。企業側は、確かな学歴を持つ従業員を雇うことができる。

　しかし、大学教育の真の目的は、従業員の提供にあるのだろうか。大学に在籍中は視野を広げることに専念すべきだという声も多い。学生は様々な本を読むことにもっと時間を割くべきだという意見もある。また、学生は批判的に考える方法を学習すべきだという意見もある。言い換えれば、自分自身で考える能力を養うため、一般教養に焦点を絞るべきだということだ。大学は潜在的従業員を訓練する場ではなく、個人を教育する場であるべきだ。

True or False 解答 & 和訳

1. T　　世界中で求人と求職者の間にギャップがある。
2. T　　学生の中には、入学試験に合格することにしか目を向けない人もいる。
3. F　　ほとんどの学生は、大学生活で何をすべきかを知っている。
4. T　　働いてくれる従業員を見つけることができない中小企業がある。
5. T　　学生たちはSTEMの分野のコースをとるよう勧められている。
6. NS　　求職者はみな大学教育を受けるべきである。

Unit 18

Have You Done Your Homework?
— 広がりつつあるデジタル教材 —

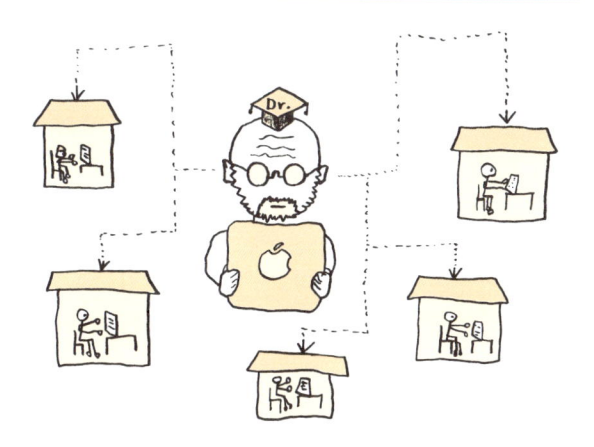

imagine	動 想像する	skip	動 読み飛ばす
present	動 見せる	highlight	動 蛍光ペンなどで塗る
material	名 教材、資料	needless to say	言うまでもなく
on top of that	それに加えて	simply	副 単に
outdated	形 古くなった	critic	名 批判する人
update	動 更新する	spy on ~	~をひそかに見張る
allow	動 可能にする	individual	形 個々の
analyze	動 分析する	fall behind	遅れを取る
appealing	形 魅力的な	assignment	名 宿題
whether	接 ~かどうか	wave of the future	将来のトレンド

Have You Done Your Homework?

Textbooks at American universities are expensive. A single textbook for a science course may cost more than $100, and that is for just one course. The average student takes four or five courses, so you can imagine how much they pay for all of their textbooks.

The publishers of university textbooks are always looking for new ways to present material. Publishers spend a lot of money to produce print textbooks, so each copy may be very expensive. On top of that, the information in print textbooks may become outdated very quickly. Therefore, publishers are now producing digital textbooks. They are cheaper and can be updated quickly.

An increasing number of university professors are choosing these digital textbooks for their courses. This allows the major publishers to collect data from thousands of students who use their digital materials. Each publisher analyzes this data to find better ways to present material and make it more appealing. But the publishers are not the only ones who are interested in using this data.

Teachers have always wanted to know whether students are reading their textbooks. Now they have a way to find out. Several publishers are offering them a special service that tells them how their students are using the textbooks. Professors can find out whether a student is skipping pages. They can find out whether a student is failing to highlight important passages in the textbook. They can even find out whether a student is taking notes. Needless to say, they also know whether a student has simply not opened the textbook at all.

Some critics say that this is spying on students. But other people say that information this data provides is very important. They say it helps professors know whether an individual student is falling behind. If a student is not reading the textbook assignments, the professor can let him know that he is not doing well in the course. Some say giving this data on student textbook use to professors is a privacy issue. But digital textbooks are clearly the wave of the future.

349 words

18 True or False?

次の 1 〜 6 の文を読み、本文の内容に合っていたら T、合わなかったら F、述べられていなかったら NS (Not stated) を選んでください。

1. **Print textbooks in American universities are rather expensive.**
   - T ☐
   - F ☐
   - NS ☐

2. **Print textbooks cannot be updated regularly or quickly.**
   - T ☐
   - F ☐
   - NS ☐

3. **Digital textbook publishers cannot get data on how students use them.**
   - T ☐
   - F ☐
   - NS ☐

4. **It is possible to know how students are using these digital textbooks.**
   - T ☐
   - F ☐
   - NS ☐

5. **Professors can learn what time of day the students are reading.**
   - T ☐
   - F ☐
   - NS ☐

6. **Digital textbooks will completely replace printed textbooks in the future.**
   - T ☐
   - F ☐
   - NS ☐

スラッシュ訳

file-36

宿題はすんだか
Have You Done Your Homework?

アメリカの大学の教科書は / 値段が高い
Textbooks at American universities / are expensive. //

1冊の教科書は / 科学のコース用の / 100ドル以上
A single textbook / for a science course / may cost

するかもしれない / そしてそれはたった1コース分だ
more than $100, / and that is for just one course. //

平均的な学生は履修する / 4、5コースを /
The average student takes / four or five courses, / so

なので、あなたは想像できるだろう / 彼らがいくら払うか / 全ての教科書に
you can imagine / how much they pay / for all of their

textbooks. //

大学用教科書の出版社は / いつも新しい
The publishers of university textbooks / are always

方法を探している / 教材を見せる
looking for new ways / to present material. //

出版社は多額の資金を費やす / 印刷された教科書を
Publishers spend a lot of money / to produce print

作るのに / なので、1冊1冊の本はとても高い
textbooks, / so each copy may be very expensive. //

それに加え / 印刷された教科書中の情報は /
On top of that, / the information in print textbooks /

すぐに古くなるかもしれない // そのため /
may become outdated very quickly. // Therefore, /

出版社は現在、デジタル版の教科書を作っている
publishers are now producing digital textbooks. //

それらは安い / そして素早く更新することができる
They are cheaper / and can be updated quickly. //

18 スラッシュ訳

増々多くの大学教員は
An increasing number of university professors / are
これらのデジタル版教科書を選んでいる / 彼らのコースに
choosing these digital textbooks / for their courses. //
これは大手の出版社を可能にする / データを集めることを /
This allows the major publishers / to collect data / from
何千もの学生から / デジタル教材を使う
thousands of students / who use their digital materials. //
それぞれの出版社が分析する / このデータを / より良い方法を見つける
Each publisher analyzes / this data / to find better
ため / 教材を見せる / そしてそれをより魅力的にする
ways / to present material / and make it more
　　　　　　　しかし出版社だけではない
appealing. // But the publishers are not the only ones /
このデータを使いたがっている人は
who are interested in using this data. //

教員は昔からずっと知りたがっていた / 学生が
Teachers have always wanted to know / whether
教科書を読んでいるかどうか / 今、彼らは方法がある
students are reading their textbooks. // Now they have a
　　/ 調べるための / いくつかの出版社は提供している
way / to find out. // Several publishers are offering them /
特別なサービスを / 彼らに教える / どのように学生が教科書を使
a special service / that tells them / how their students
っているのか / 大学教員は調べることができる /
are using the textbooks. // Professors can find out /
学生がページを読み飛ばしているかどうか / 彼らは調べることがで
whether a student is skipping pages. // They can find
きる / 学生がしそこなっているかどうか / 重要な段落に蛍光ペンで印を
out / whether a student is failing / to highlight important
つけることを / 教科書中の / 彼らは調べることができる
passages / in the textbook. // They can even find out /

whether a student is taking notes. ∥ Needless to say, / they also know / whether a student has simply not opened the textbook at all. ∥

　Some critics say / that this is spying on students. ∥ But other people say / that information this data provides / is very important. ∥ They say / it helps professors know / whether an individual student is falling behind. ∥ If a student is not reading the textbook assignments, / the professor can let him know / that he is not doing well / in the course. ∥ Some say / giving this data on student textbook use / to professors / is a privacy issue. ∥ But digital textbooks / are clearly the wave of the future. ∥

18 和訳 & 解答

宿題はすんだか

　アメリカの大学の教科書は高価だ。科学系のコースでは教科書1冊が100ドルを超える場合もあり、それはしかもたった1コースでの話だ。平均的な学生は4、5コースをとるので、全ての教科書にいくら払っているか想像できるだろう。

　大学用教科書の出版社は、教材を提示する新しい方法を常に模索している。出版社は印刷された教科書の作成に多額の費用をかけるので、1冊の価格は非常に高くなることがある。そのうえ、印刷された教科書の情報はまたたく間に古くなるおそれがある。それゆえ、出版社は今ではデジタル版の教科書を作成している。デジタル版の教科書のほうが安価で、素早く更新できる。

　コースにデジタル版教科書を使用する大学教員も増えている。これにより、大手出版社は自社のデジタル教材を使用する何千人もの学生からデータを集めることができる。各出版社は、教材のより良い提示の仕方を見つけるため、そして魅力的なものにするため、このデータを分析する。しかし、このデータを使いたがっているのは出版社だけではない。

　教師は常に、学生が教科書を読んでいるかどうか知りたがっていたが、今やそれを知る方法があるのだ。いくつかの出版社は、学生がどのように教科書を使用しているかを教師に知らせる特別なサービスを提供している。教師は、ある学生がページを読み飛ばしたかどうか調べることができる。学生が教科書の重要な一節にマーカーを入れそこねたことも、メモをとっているかどうかもわかる。言うまでもなく、学生が単にまったく教科書を開かなかったこともわかる。

　これは学生を監視する行為だと批判する声もあるが、このデータから得られる情報は非常に重要だという人々もいる。教員にとって、個々の学生が授業に遅れを取っていないかを知る助けになるというのだ。もし学生が教科書の課題を読んでいないなら、教員は彼がコースを順調にこなしていないと知らせることができる。学生の教科書使用に関するデータを教員に提供するのは、プライバシーの問題だという意見もある。しかし、デジタル版教科書は明らかに今後、増える傾向にあるだろう。

True or False　解答 & 和訳

1. T　アメリカの大学の紙の教科書は、値段がかなり高い。
2. NS　定期的に、あるいは素早く紙の教科書を更新することはできない。
3. F　デジタル版教科書の出版社は、学生の教科書使用法に関するデータを得ることはできない。
4. T　学生がこれらのデジタル版教科書をどのように使っているかを知ることができる。
5. NS　教員は、学生が一日のうちいつ読者をしているかを知ることができる。
6. NS　紙の教科書は、今後完全にデジタル版にとって代わるだろう。

Unit 19

The Ideal Translator
― 自動翻訳の開発とその限界 ―

rapidly	副 急激に	decide	動 決める
translate	動 翻訳する	automatically	副 自動的に
machine translation	機械翻訳	limited	形 限りのある
follow	動 従う	subject matter	題材
exception	名 例外	unlimited	形 限りのない
therefore	副 従って	failure	名 失敗
rule-based	形 規則に基づいた	pen	名 (家畜の)囲い
based on ~	~に基づいた	on the basis of ~	~に基づいて
match	動 照合させる	refer to ~	~を示す
in order to ~	~するため	helpful	形 役立つ

19 速読

The Ideal Translator

The need to communicate with people in other languages is increasing rapidly. Learning a foreign language can be exciting. But it takes a lot of time and effort. It would be great to have software that would translate from one language to another. Machine translation (MT) could save a lot of time, energy and stress.

For years, companies and governments have been trying to produce such MT software. Some of these software programs are based on grammar rules. But we don't always follow these rules when we speak and write. There are also lots of exceptions. Therefore, rule-based MT is not very successful.

Another variety of software is based on translations that have been done before. This matches original texts and translated texts in a database in order to decide the best fit. It takes a Japanese sentence and automatically translates it into an English sentence. The problem is how to decide which possible translation is the best one. That is hard for humans to decide, but it is even harder for machines.

MT software programs have been successful with limited subject matter. One example is weather information. The vocabulary is limited, and the grammar is limited. Therefore, a Japanese-language weather forecast can be translated into clear English easily.

But MT software has not been successful with subject matter that is unlimited. An example is the failure to correctly translate the following two sentences: "The pen is in the box" and "The box is in the pen." The key is that "pen" has several meanings. It usually means something to write with, but a pen is also a fence to keep animals in. Humans understand these sentences on the basis of experience in the real world. Context tells them that the first sentence refers to a pen-size box and the second sentence refers to a pen to keep pigs or sheep in.

This does not mean MT is not helpful. MT can be quite helpful as a tool in the process of translating. But in the end, the human ability to think is essential in the process of translating.

352 words

19 True or False?

次の 1 〜 6 の文を読み、本文の内容に合っていたら T、合わなかったら F、述べられていなかったら NS (Not stated) を選んでください。

1. Machine translation could make learning foreign languages unnecessary.
   - T ☐
   - F ☐
   - NS ☐

2. MT software does not use rules of grammar.
   - T ☐
   - F ☐
   - NS ☐

3. It is not easy to know which translation is best.
   - T ☐
   - F ☐
   - NS ☐

4. Weather information is the only subject matter that is limited.
   - T ☐
   - F ☐
   - NS ☐

5. In the example, the word "pen" has two different meanings.
   - T ☐
   - F ☐
   - NS ☐

6. Machine translation should not be used as a tool.
   - T ☐
   - F ☐
   - NS ☐

スラッシュ訳

理想的な翻訳者
The Ideal Translator

The need to communicate with people / in other languages / is increasing rapidly. // Learning a foreign language can be exciting. // But it takes a lot of time and effort. // It would be great to have software / that would translate from one language to another. //

Machine translation (MT) could save / a lot of time, energy and stress. //

For years, / companies and governments have been trying / to produce such MT software. // Some of these software programs / are based on grammar rules. // But we don't always follow these rules / when we speak and write. // There are also lots of exceptions. // Therefore, / rule-based MT is not very successful. //

19 スラッシュ訳

Another variety of software / is based on translations / that have been done before. // This matches / original texts and translated texts / in a database / in order to decide the best fit. // It takes a Japanese sentence / and automatically translates it / into an English sentence. // The problem is / how to decide / which possible translation is the best one. // That is hard / for humans to decide, / but it is even harder / for machines. //

MT software programs have been successful / with limited subject matter. // One example is weather information. // The vocabulary is limited, / and the grammar is limited. // Therefore, / a Japanese-language weather forecast can be translated / into clear English / easily. //

But MT software has not been successful / with

subject matter that is unlimited. An example is the failure to correctly translate the following two sentences: "The pen is in the box" and "The box is in the pen." The key is that "pen" has several meanings. It usually means something to write with, but a pen is also a fence to keep animals in. Humans understand these sentences on the basis of experience in the real world. Context tells them that the first sentence refers to a pen-size box and the second sentence refers to a pen to keep pigs or sheep in.

This does not mean MT is not helpful. MT can be quite helpful as a tool in the process of translating. But in the end, the human ability to think is essential in the process of translating.

19 和訳 & 解答

理想的な翻訳者

　言語の異なる人々同士のコミュニケーションの必要性が急速に高まっている。外国語の習得は楽しい面もあるものの、多くの時間と努力を要する。ひとつの言語を別の言語に翻訳するソフトがあったら素晴らしいだろう。機械翻訳（MT）があれば、多くの時間、エネルギーとストレスを省くことができる。

　長年の間、企業と政府はそういったMTソフトの製作に取り組んできた。これらのソフトウエアプログラムには文法規則に基づいたものもあるが、人は文法規則どおりに話したり書いたりするとは限らないし、例外も多い。そのため、文法規則に基づいたMTはあまり成果をあげていない。

　別の種類のソフトは、過去の翻訳例に基づいているものがある。これはデータベース内で原文と訳文を照合させて、一番合致する訳文を決定する。ひとつの和文を自動的に英文に翻訳する。問題は、訳の候補の中からどうやって最適な翻訳を決めるかだ。人間にとっても難しいが、機械にとってはなおさらだ。

　MTソフトウエアプログラムは、限られた題材においては上手くいっている。例えば気象情報だ。使う用語も文法も限られているので、日本語の天気予報を明快な英語に翻訳することはたやすい。

　しかし、MTソフトは題材が限定されていない場合には上手くいかない。ひとつ例をあげると、次の二つの文を正しく訳すことができない。「The pen is in the box.（ペンが箱の中にある）」と「The box is in the pen.（箱が囲いの中にある）」である。鍵は「pen」が多義語であるということだ。普通は「pen」といえば書くために使う物のことだが、家畜を入れておく囲いの意味もあるのだ。人間は実世界での経験に基づいて文意を理解する。文脈から、最初の文が言っているのはペンが入る大きさの箱のことで、二番目の文では豚や羊を入れる囲いのことだとわかる。

　MTが役に立たないことはない。MTは、翻訳の過程におけるツールとしては、非常に役に立つこともある。しかし結局は、人間の思考能力が翻訳の過程に不可欠だ。

True or False　解答 & 和訳

1. F　機械翻訳は、外国語学習を不要にすることができるだろう。
2. F　機械翻訳ソフトは、文法のルールを使っていない。
3. T　どちらの訳が最も良いか判断するのは容易ではない。
4. NS　天気予報は、唯一の限定的な題材だ。
5. T　例の中で、penという単語は2つの違った意味を持つ。
6. F　機械翻訳は、道具として使われるべきではない。

Unit 20

Speaking Two Languages
― 子供とバイリンガル ―

mother baby greys

amazing	形 見事な	minus	名 欠点、デメリット
recognize	動 認識する	in the long run	長い目で見れば
respond to ~	~に反応する	catch up with ~	~に追いつく
encourage	動 ~するように働きかける	benefit	名 利益
gradually	副 少しずつ	accuracy	名 正確性
tend to ~	~する傾向がある	in addition	さらに
social skill	社会的能力	experience	動 経験する
stimulate	動 刺激する	age-related	形 加齢に伴う
beneficial	形 利益がある	dementia	名 認知症
plus	名 利点、メリット	advantage	名 有利な点

Speaking Two Languages

The human brain is amazing. From the moment a child is born, it can hear spoken words. Slowly it begins to recognize combinations of sounds as language. Sounds of any language are okay. If the child hears Japanese, then it begins to recognize the sounds of that language. If the child hears English, then it begins to recognize the sounds of English.

By the time the child reaches nine months of age, it produces sounds from hundreds of languages. Parents respond to selected sounds and that encourages the child to use those sounds again and again. During the first six years of life, the child learns about three new words a day. During its lifetime, that child will grow up and gradually master some 50,000 words in one language.

What happens if a child has to learn two languages? Some researchers say bilingual kids learn faster. These kids tend to do well in school. They seem to develop social skills a little faster. These researchers think learning two languages stimulates the brain in more ways than one language does.

Other researchers, however, find that bilingualism is not always beneficial. Bilingual kids understand a smaller number of words than kids using just one language. Later they produce a smaller number of words. Perhaps parents mix words from the two languages. They may choose words they feel their children will more easily understand. One example is "Japlish," a combination of Japanese and English words.

There are pluses and minuses in growing up as a bilingual person. But in the long run, bilingual kids catch up with kids who speak only one language. They usually use both languages well, if not perfectly. Learning two languages early in life can also have benefits later in life. In 2013 a study was made of people who spoke one language and bilingual people in the 60 to 68-year-old age group. Both groups performed tasks with the same accuracy. But the bilinguals were faster and their brains used less energy to do the tasks. In addition, bilinguals experience age-related dementia later than people who speak only one language. Even in old age, speaking two languages has advantages.

363 words

20 True or False?

次の1～6の文を読み、本文の内容に合っていたらT、合わなかったらF、述べられていなかったらNS（Not stated）を選んでください。

1	From birth, a child can hear only certain kinds of words.	T ☐ F ☐ NS ☐
2	A Japanese child cannot recognize English words.	T ☐ F ☐ NS ☐
3	Between birth and age six, a child learns about three words per day.	T ☐ F ☐ NS ☐
4	Bilingual kids learn double the number of words learned by kids using one language.	T ☐ F ☐ NS ☐
5	Bilingual kids eventually use the two languages well.	T ☐ F ☐ NS ☐
6	Being bilingual has advantages even when one reaches the age of 60.	T ☐ F ☐ NS ☐

スラッシュ訳

file-40

二つの言語を話す
Speaking Two Languages

The human brain is amazing. // From the moment / a child is born, / it can hear spoken words. // Slowly it begins to recognize / combinations of sounds / as language. // Sounds of any language / are okay. // If the child hears Japanese, / then it begins to recognize / the sounds of that language. // If the child hears English, / then it begins to recognize / the sounds of English. //

By the time the child reaches nine months of age, / it produces sounds / from hundreds of languages. // Parents respond to selected sounds / and that encourages the child / to use those sounds / again and again. // During the first six years of life, / the child learns / about three new words / a day. // During

20 スラッシュ訳

its lifetime, / that child will grow up / and gradually
master / some 50,000 words / in one language. //
What happens / if a child has to learn two languages? //
Some researchers say / bilingual kids learn faster. //
These kids tend to / do well / in school. // They seem /
to develop social skills / a little faster. // These researchers
think / learning two languages / stimulates
the brain / in more ways / than one language does. //
Other researchers, / however, / find / that
bilingualism is not always beneficial. / Bilingual kids
understand / a smaller number of words / than kids
using just one language. // Later they produce / a
smaller number of words. // Perhaps parents mix words /
from the two languages. // They may choose words /
they feel / their children will more easily understand. //
One example is "Japlish," / a combination of Japanese

and English words.

There are pluses and minuses in growing up as a bilingual person. But in the long run, bilingual kids catch up with kids who speak only one language. They usually use both languages well, if not perfectly. Learning two languages early in life can also have benefits later in life. In 2013 a study was made of people who spoke one language and bilingual people in the 60 to 68-year-old age group. Both groups performed tasks with the same accuracy. But the bilinguals were faster and their brains used less energy to do the tasks. In addition, bilinguals experience age-related dementia later than people who speak only one language. Even in old age, speaking two languages has advantages.

20 和訳 & 解答

二つの言語を話す

　人間の脳は素晴らしい。赤ん坊は産まれた瞬間からもう人間の話す言葉を聞くことができる。そして徐々に音の組合せを認識し始める。どんな言語でも聞き取れる。子どもは日本語を聞けば日本語の音を、英語を聞けば英語の音を認識し始める。

　子どもが生後9カ月になる頃には、何百もの言語の音声を発するようになる。親が特定の音に反応し、それは子どもがその音を繰り返し使うことを促すことになる。人生の最初の6年間、子どもは1日につきおよそ三つの新しい単語を学ぶ。生涯を通して、子どもは成長し、徐々にひとつの言語で約5万語を習得する。

　もし子どもが二つの言語をおぼえる必要があったらどうなるだろう。バイリンガルの子どもは学習が早いと言う研究者もいる。これらの子どもは学校でも良い成績を修める傾向があり、社会的能力の発達も少々速いようだ。研究者は、ひとつの言語を学ぶよりも、ふたつの言語を学ぶ方がさまざまな面で脳を刺激するのだと考えている。

　しかし、二つの言語を話すことが必ずしも有益でないと考える研究者もいる。バイリンガルの子どもは、ひとつの言語を使う子どもよりも理解する単語数が少なく、成長しても使える語彙がより狭くなる。おそらく、親は二つの言語の言葉を混ぜて使うのだろう。子どもにわかりやすいと思う単語を選んでいるのかもしれない。英語と日本語の組み合わせである「Japlish」はそういった例のひとつだ。

　バイリンガルとして育つことには長所も短所もあるが、長い目で見ると、バイリンガルの子どもは、ひとつの言語だけを話す子どもに追いつく。大抵は両方の言語を、完璧ではないにしても最終的に上手に使いこなす。幼少時に二つの言語を学ぶことは、老年期になっても利益をもたらすことがある。2013年に、ひとつの言語しか話さない人々とバイリンガルの人々の、60歳から68歳のグループに対する研究が行われた。どちらのグループも、課題をこなす正確さは変わらなかったが、バイリンガルの人々のほうがより迅速に課題をこなし、脳のエネルギー消費量も少なかった。これに加え、バイリンガルは、ひとつの言語だけを話す人々よりも老年期の認知症を経験するのが遅い。老年期にさえ、二つの言語を話すことには利点があるのだ。

True or False　解答 & 和訳

1. F　　生後、子どもはある種類の言葉だけを聞くことができる。
2. F　　日本人の子どもは、英語の言葉を認識できない。
3. T　　生後から6歳までの間、子どもは1日につき約3つ新しい単語を覚える。
4. NS　バイリンガルの子どもは、ひとつの言語を使う子どもの倍の単語を覚える。
5. T　　バイリンガルの子どもは、最終的に二つの言語を上手に使う。
6. T　　バイリンガルであることは、60歳の年齢に達するときでもなお、有利である。

＋ カポーティに触れる

The Headless Hawk

Vincent switched off the lights in the gallery. Outside, after locking the door, he smoothed the brim of an elegant Panama, and started toward Third Avenue, his umbrella-cane tap-tap-tapping along the pavement. A promise of rain had darkened the day since dawn, and a sky of bloated clouds blurred the five o'clock sun; it was hot, though, humid as tropical mist, and voices, sounding along the gray July street, sounding muffed and strange, carried a fretful undertone. Vincent felt as though he moved below the sea. ………

THE COMPLETE STORIES OF TRUMAN CAPOTE
TRUMAN CAPOTE
VINTAGE INTERNATIONAL

英語のリズム、流れ。高校生だった村上春樹さんが感嘆したのもうなずけます。
村上さんは、長じて、カポーティの文章に負けないすばらしい日本語翻訳をされました。その作品は『誕生日の子どもたち』(文藝春秋) に「無頭の鷹」というタイトルで収録されています。ご興味がある方はぜひ手にとってみてください。
村上さんの翻訳と、ご自分で翻訳したものと比べてみるのもいいでしょう。
また新たな好奇心が生まれるかもしれません。

著者紹介

James M. Vardaman　ジェームス・M・バーダマン

1947年、アメリカ、テネシー生まれ。ハワイ大学アジア研究専攻、修士。早稲田大学文化構想学部教授。著書に『毎日の英文法　頭の中に「英語のパターン」をつくる』『毎日の英単語　日常頻出語の90％をマスターする』(小社)、『アメリカの小学生が学ぶ歴史教科書』(ジャパンブック)、『アメリカ南部』(講談社)、『黒人差別とアメリカ公民権運動』(集英社新書)、『もう一つのアメリカ史』(東京書籍)など多数ある。

神崎　正哉　かんざき・まさや

1967年、神奈川県生まれ。神田外語大学講師。東京水産大学(現東京海洋大学)海洋環境工学科卒。テンプル大学大学院修士課程修了(英語教授法)。TOEIC®テスト990点、TOEIC®SW200点/200点(TOEIC®4技能合計1390点)、英検1級、国連英検特A級、ケンブリッジ英検CPEなど英語の資格多数。著書に『新TOEIC® TEST　出る順で学ぶボキャブラリー』(講談社)、共著書に『1駅1題!　新TOEIC© TEST 「読解」特急』(小社)など多数ある。

毎日の英速読
頭の中に「英文解読の回路」をつくる

2014年 6 月30日　第1刷発行
2021年 9 月20日　第16刷発行

著者　James M. Vardaman　神崎　正哉
装丁・ブックデザイン　寄藤文平＋杉山健太郎(文平銀座)
発行者　三宮博信
発行所　朝日新聞出版
　　　　〒104-8011　東京都中央区築地5-3-2
電話　　03-5541-8814(編集)
　　　　03-5540-7793(販売)
印刷所　大日本印刷株式会社
©2014 James M. Vardaman, Kanzaki Masaya
Published in Japan by Asahi Shimbun Publications Inc.
ISBN 978-4-02-331284-5
定価はカバーに表示してあります。
本書掲載の文章・図版の無断複写・転載を禁じます。
落丁・乱丁の場合は弊社業務部(電話03-5540-7800)へご連絡ください。
送料弊社負担にてお取り替えいたします。